King David and His Psalms

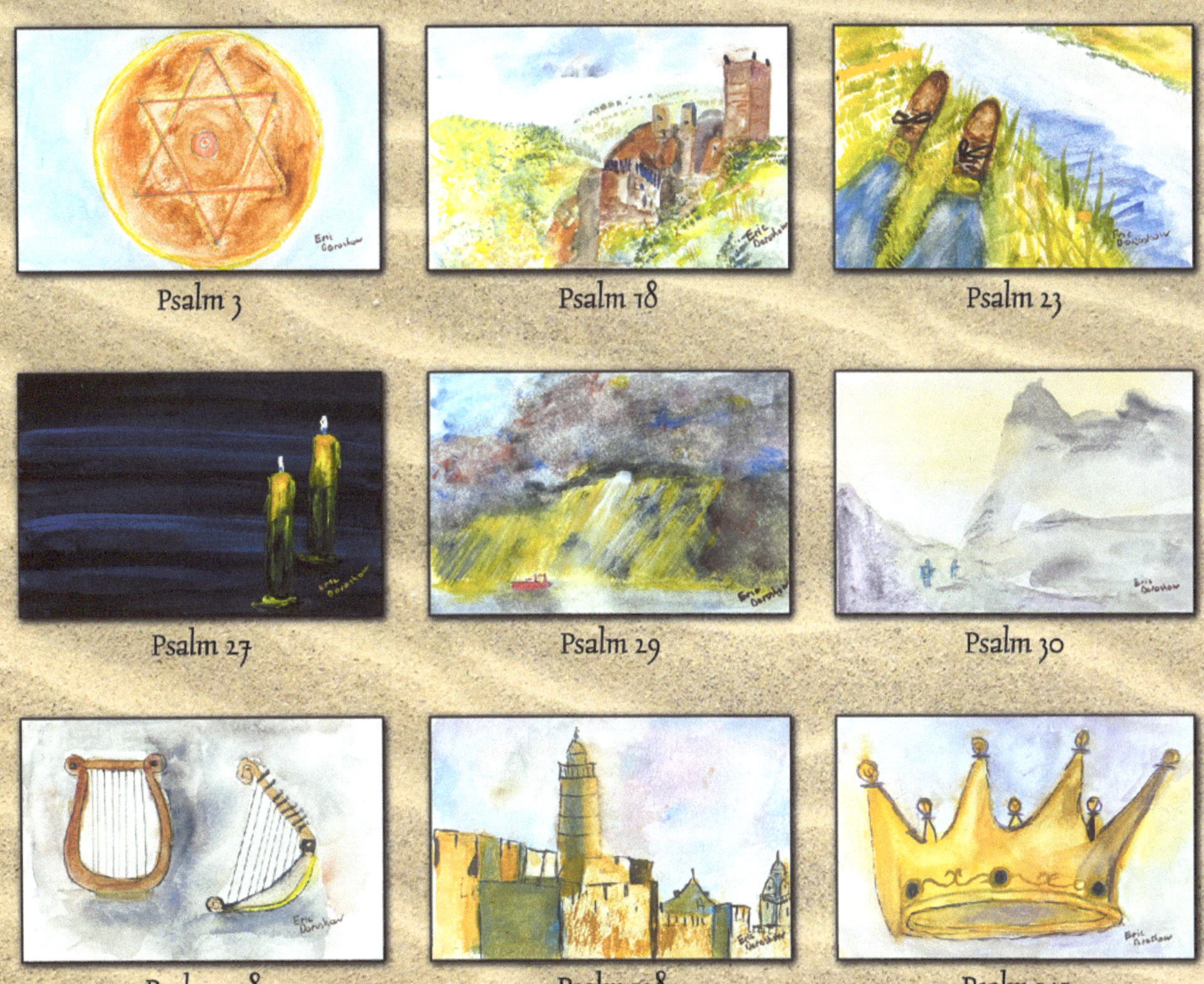

Psalm 3 | Psalm 18 | Psalm 23

Psalm 27 | Psalm 29 | Psalm 30

Psalm 108 | Psalm 138 | Psalm 145

KING DAVID AND HIS PSALMS

LESSONS OF COURAGE AND INSPIRATION
FOR TODAY'S TOUGH TIMES

ERIC M. DOROSHOW
ARTIST · AUTHOR

King David and His Psalms:
Lessons of Courage and Inspiration
for Today's Tough Times

All Watercolor Artwork by
Eric Doroshow

Paintings by Eric Doroshow

ISBN: 979-8-218-09867-4

Weldin Park Associates LLC
1202 Kirkwood Highway
Wilmington, DE 19805

Israel Photographs Courtesy of Unsplash:

And David said to his son Solomon, "Be strong and of good courage and do not fear and be not dismayed, for the Lord G-d, my G-d, is with you. He will not fail you or forsake you till all the work on the House of the Lord is done."

I CHRONICLES 28:20

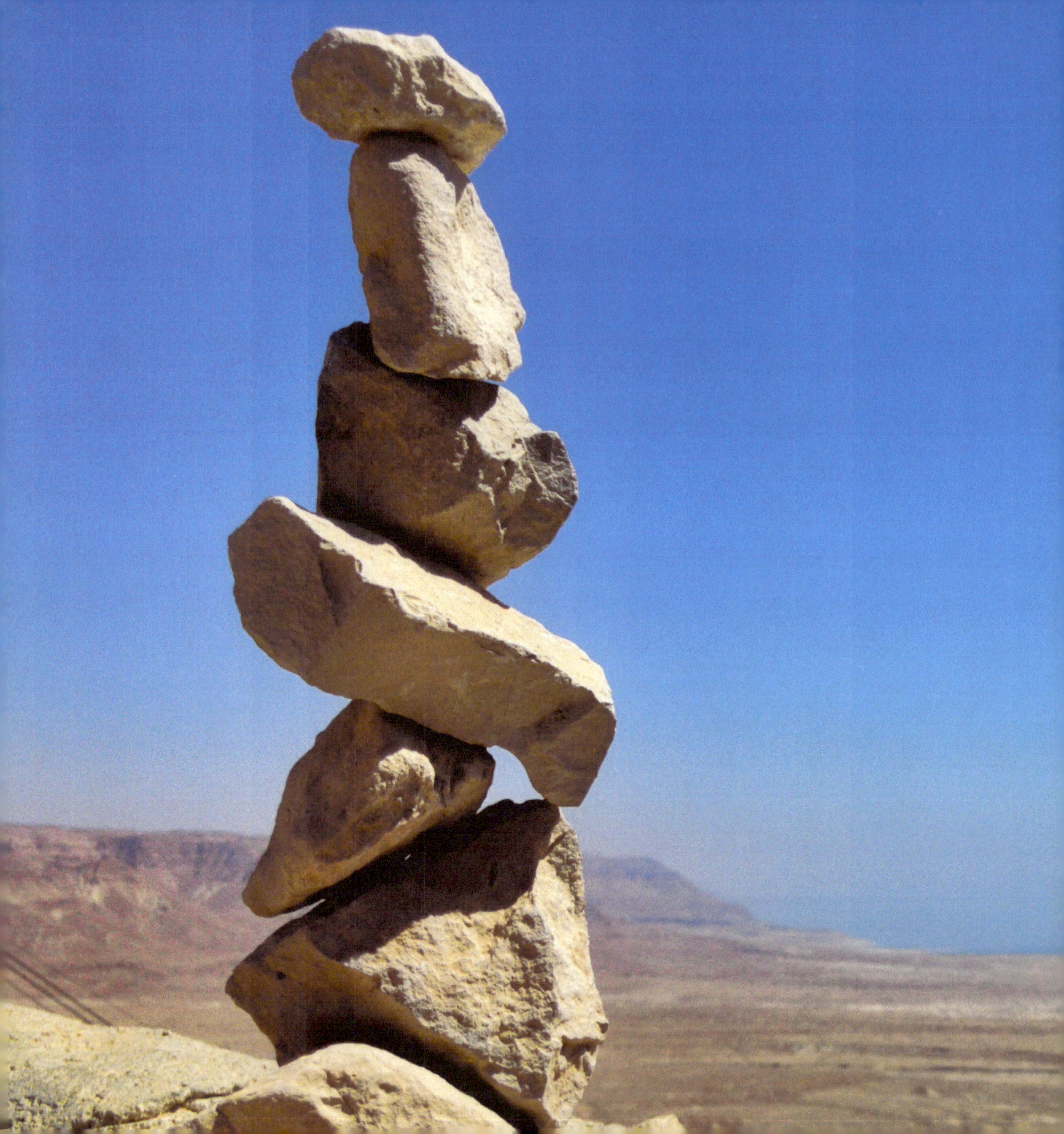

Table of Contents

PREFACE i

CHAPTER ONE 1
A Short History of The Twelve Tribes Of Israel Until The Time of King David

CHAPTER TWO 7
A Short History of King David and His Reign

CHAPTER THREE 17
King David And Courage

CHAPTER FOUR 31
King David And Christianity

CHAPTER FIVE 35
King David And Islam

CHAPTER SIX 41
King David And Judaism

CHAPTER SEVEN 47
King David And Leadership

CHAPTER EIGHT 55
The Archeological Debate About King David

CHAPTER NINE 61
The Psalms of David

CHAPTER TEN 107
Why David's Story Is Relevant To Us Today

CONCLUSION 117

וישאו בני ישראל את עיניהם
והנה מצרים נסע אחריהם ויראו מאד
ויצעקו בני ישראל אל יהוה
ויאמרו אל משה המבלי אין קברים
במצרים לקחתנו
מה זאת עשית לנו להוציאנו ממצרים
הלא זה הדבר אשר דברנו אליך
במצרים לאמר חדל ממנו ונעבדה
את מצרים כי טוב לנו עבד את מצרים
ויאמר משה אל העם
אל תיראו התיצבו וראו את ישועת יהוה
אשר יעשה לכם היום כי אשר ראיתם
את מצרים היום לא תספו לראתם עוד עד
עולם יהוה ילחם לכם ואתם תחרשון

מי כמכה נאדר בקדש
פלא
נטית ימינך
נחית בחסדך עם זו גאלת
שמעו עמים
חיל אחז ישבי פלשת
אז נבהלו אלופי אדום
אילי מואב יאחזמו
נמגו כל ישבי כנען
ופחד
בגדל זרועך ידמו כ
עד יעבר עמך יהוה
קנית
תבאמו ותטעמו בהר נחלתך
לשבתך פעלת יהוה
ידיך
יהוה ימלך לעלם ועד
כי בא סוס פרעה ברכבו ובפרשיו בים
את מי הים
ובני ישראל הלכו ביבשה
ותקח מרים הנביאה אחות אהרן את התף בידה
אחריה בתפים ובמחלת ותען להם מרים
סוס ורכבו רמה בים
ויצאו אל מדבר שור וילכו
ויבאו מרתה ולא יכלו לשתת
שמה מרה
יהוה ויורהו

PREFACE

TODAY'S CURRENT events have shaken us to the core. First came the COVID pandemic. Our world changed overnight. Lockdowns and social distancing became routine. The workplace became time at home for another Zoom meeting, while school became time at home for another Zoom session for our children. We longed for direct contact with others. Some friends and relatives became infected and very sick from COVID. Some even died from it.

We felt frustrated and powerless. Even the simplest activities of daily living, like going to the grocery store, had to be carefully choreographed. Our fondest hope was just to have our normal lives back again.

Just as we thought we were reclaiming some post-pandemic normalcy, we suddenly faced unprecedented spikes in inflation. It was the highest inflation rate in 40 years. To make matters worse, we got hit with supply chain problems, which resulted in extended delays for consumer goods that used to be delivered in just days.

Then came the invasion of Ukraine, which was the largest European land war since World War II. We saw death, destruction, and suffering on a scale we could scarcely imagine.

Suddenly, the scariest part of the day became the time we spent watching the nightly news on TV.

These events have forced us to deal with a new normal in our lives. The world has been permanently changed. Our old ways of doing things have quickly become obsolete. Other than hearing that "we are all in this together," we received little guidance about how we should approach these dramatic life changes.

With so much misery, death, and destruction seen on a daily basis, many of us desperately seek the guidance to confront these unprecedented challenges. But where can we find this guidance?

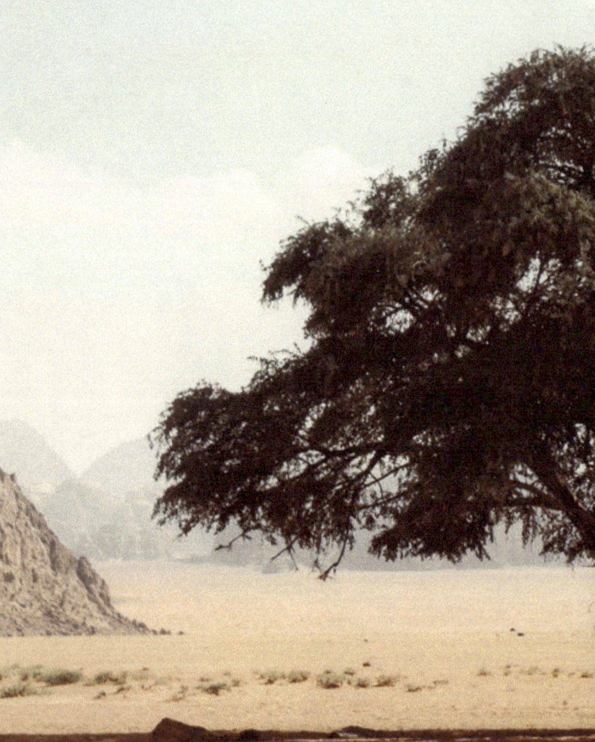

I believe the guidance for today can be found in the story of someone who lived thousands of years ago. The life lessons and Psalms of King David have real meaning as we struggle to deal with today's unprecedented challenges.

David is venerated in the three great Abrahamic religions of the world. In Judaism, David is known as the King of Israel. In Christianity, Jesus is described as having descended from him. In Islam, David is described as a major prophet. David's 75 Psalms soar with inspiration, emotion, and reverence. They are a cornerstone of the liturgy of not only Judaism, but also of Christianity and Islam.

David has inspired many works of Jewish and Christian art. Many famous painters painted David through the centuries. For instance, one of Titian's most famous works is his painting of David in battle against Goliath. In early Hebrew manuscripts, we see David wearing a crown and playing the lyre. In ancient manuscripts from Byzantine times, we learn that David was an ancestor of Jesus. One of the most famous artistic depictions of David is the David sculpture

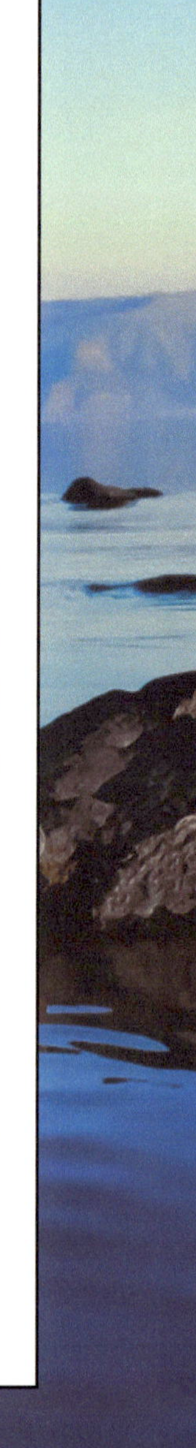

by Michelangelo. Created between 1501 and 1504, this sculpture is considered a masterpiece of Renaissance sculpture. It is a marble statue of David and stands majestically at 17 feet. The sculpture is a favored subject by art patrons who visit Florence, Italy.

David's life is full of contradictions. It contains many inspiring stories that soar and represent the best of humanity, and yet there are some stories that show humanity's dark side. Both are helpful in giving us guidance today.

I began my own journey to learn about King David by reading the Davidic Psalms. I then chose my nine favorite Psalms of David and painted a 6" by 9" watercolor representing an important theme for each of these nine Psalms. Originally, this book was to be limited to a discussion of just these nine Davidic Psalms. But as I read more about King David, I felt I had to do more. Although the Psalms are awe-inspiring, I felt that there was even more to the story of King David than just his Psalms. I began looking closely at the stories of his life to see what guidance they can provide us today.

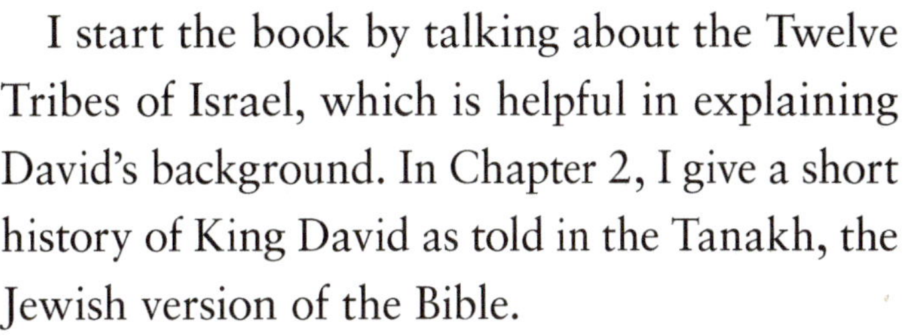

I start the book by talking about the Twelve Tribes of Israel, which is helpful in explaining David's background. In Chapter 2, I give a short history of King David as told in the Tanakh, the Jewish version of the Bible.

I found many stories of strength of courage in David's life that we can apply to today. In Chapter 3, I discuss some of the more significant stories about David's acts of courage.

In Chapter 4, I discuss King David and Christianity. Special thanks to Pastor Daniel Nelms of Wilmington, DE, who helped guide me in writing this chapter. In Chapter 5, I write about King David and Islam. Special thanks to Imam Arqum Rashid of Wilmington, DE for his assistance in writing this chapter. In Chapter 6, I write about King David and Judaism. Special thanks go to Rabbi Steven Saks for his help and guidance in writing this chapter. In addition to speaking to these leaders of the three Abrahamic religions, I reviewed several Christian, Islam, and Jewish texts to learn about each religion's perspective on King David.

In Chapter 7, I write about King David and

leadership. Here, I used some of the topics discussed in Richard D. Phillips' 1999 book entitled *The Heart of an Executive*. The author states that David's story is one of a supreme career executive. He suggests that today's executives can learn many important lessons from the trials and triumphs of David.

Before I wrote Chapter 8 on King David and Archeology, I read numerous articles describing several recent archeological findings about King David. These articles include an excellent one by Ruth Margalit entitled "In Search of King David's Lost Empire", published in the June 22, 2020 issue of *The New Yorker* magazine. I also reviewed several articles on this topic published in the Israeli newspaper *Haaretz*. Through these sources I learned about a bitter debate among archeologists on whether King David actually existed. In Chapter 8, I discuss this debate, as well as some exciting new archeological discoveries about King David.

In Chapter 9, I delve into nine of David's most poetic and meaningful Psalms. First, each Psalm is recounted in its entirety. Then, I discuss the essence of these nine Psalms. Finally, I use my original watercolors to help convey the inspirational message of each Psalm.

In Chapter 10, I discuss how David's story is relevant to us today. David demonstrated several important precepts which we can apply in our current struggles in order to live a more meaningful life. These precepts include perseverance, courage, humility, truthfulness, equanimity, gratitude, responsibility, and order.

Some of my research about King David is derived from the Jewish books of the Tanakh, including I Samuel, II Samuel, I Kings, and I Chronicles. *The Encyclopedia Judaic*a (1972 edition) and the Jewish Virtual Library were invaluable resources.

Let us begin our journey together as we learn more about King David and his Psalms. My hope is that we will gain courage and inspiration from these stories.

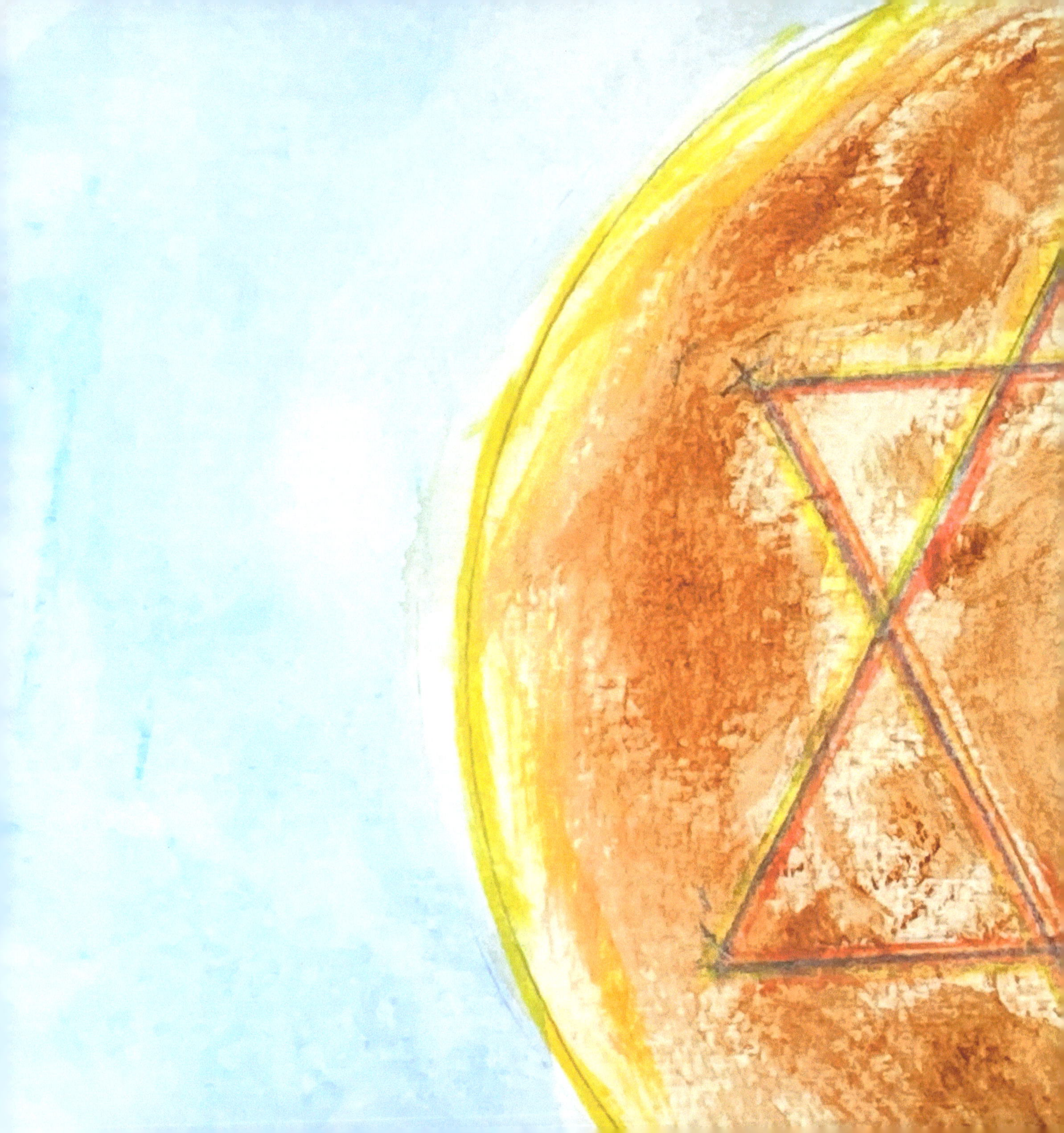

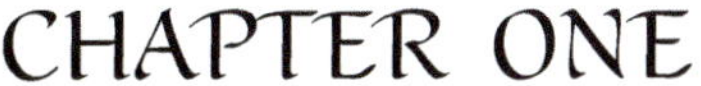

CHAPTER ONE

A Short History of The Twelve Tribes Of Israel Until The Time of King David

AS WE SHALL SEE, David eventually became the second king of the Twelve Tribes of Israel. But what are the Twelve Tribes? Where did they come from? Before we talk about the life of King David, it will be helpful to learn more about the tribes.

The story of the Twelve Tribes of Israel, collectively called Israel, is told in detail in the Bible. Biblical tradition holds that the tribes are descended from the sons and grandsons of Jacob. G-d made Himself known to Moses and rescued the Israelites from an oppressive pharaoh in Egypt. At Mount Sinai, the nation received its laws and made a covenant with G-d. After wandering for 40 years in the desert, the Twelve

Tribes were blessed by Jacob and Moses in Genesis and Deuteronomy. According to commentary by Jean Leymarie in her book, *The Jerusalem Windows:*

> Jacob called to his side his twelve sons (who gave their names to the twelve tribes) and blessed each, calling each by name and revealing his nature and destiny.
>
> The dying Moses repeated Jacob's solemn act and in a somewhat different order, also blessed the twelve tribes of Israel who were about to enter the land of Canaan.

The twelve tribes were Asher, Benjamin, Dan, Gad, Issachar, Joseph, Judah, Levi, Naphtali, Reuben, Simeon, and Zebulun.

Modern scholarship is conflicted about much of the history of the tribes. Nevertheless, it appears that their covenant with G-d, their common history, and their common religion bound them together. Each tribe was made up of several clans, although the tribe of Dan supposedly consisted of a single clan.

Before the Kings of Israel, each tribe was ruled by a Judge who often was the elder of the clan.

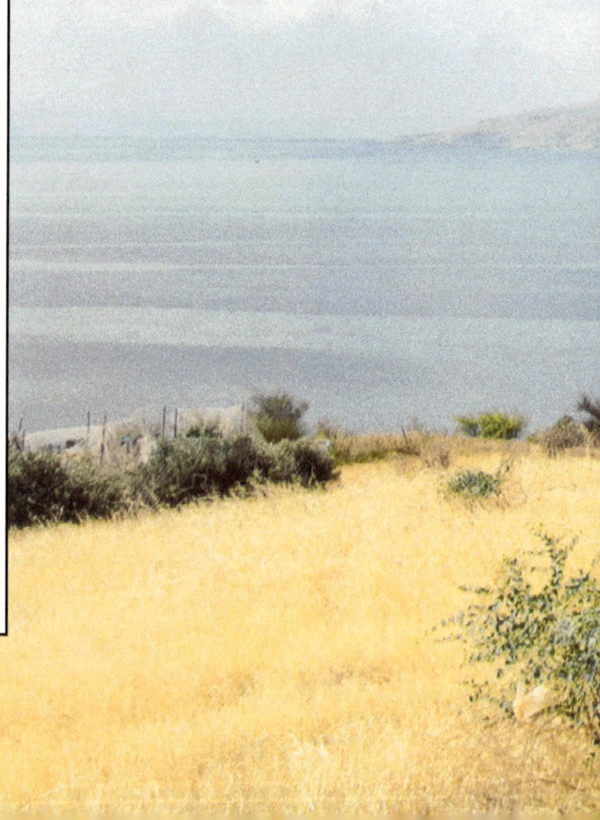

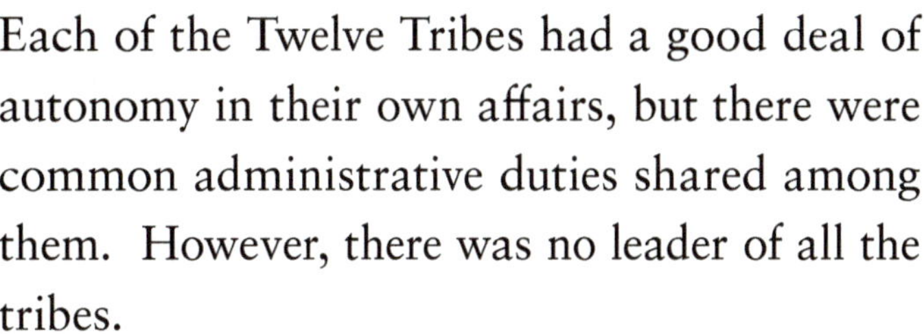

Each of the Twelve Tribes had a good deal of autonomy in their own affairs, but there were common administrative duties shared among them. However, there was no leader of all the tribes.

The tribes invaded Canaan with Joshua in command. They united and conquered the land, which was then divided among them. However, the tribe of Levi received no land, as "the priesthood of the LORD is their inheritance" Joshua 18:7. When Levi is counted among the Twelve Tribes, the Joseph tribes are counted as one. However, when Levi is not mentioned, the Joseph tribe is split in two between Joseph's sons and counted separately as Manasseh and Ephraim.

The war against Nahash the Ammonite showed that the tribes came to their mutual military aid if any one of the tribes had difficulty. In one case, unified action by the tribes was started against the Tribe of Benjamin for a breach of the terms of the covenant.

However, The Song of Deborah in Judges 5 gives clear evidence that there was some lack of military solidarity among the tribes. Praiseworthy are Ephraim, Benjamin, Manasseh, Zebulun, Issachar, and Naphtali. Discredited are the tribes of Reuben, Gad, Dan, and Asher. Judah and Simeon are not mentioned.

Some of the tribes worked together in nonmilitary matters. For example, the tribe of Zebulun engaged in trade and supported the tribe of Issachar. This was done to enable the members of Issachar to devote themselves to the study of the Torah.

Each tribe had a flag of a different color, corresponding to the stone on Aaron's breastplate.

Eventually, the tribes were compelled to find a King. I Samuel 11:15. Israel's first King was Saul. But as we shall see in chapter 2, Saul had many flaws which resulted in a failed reign. His failures paved the way for David to be King over all the tribes.

NOTES:

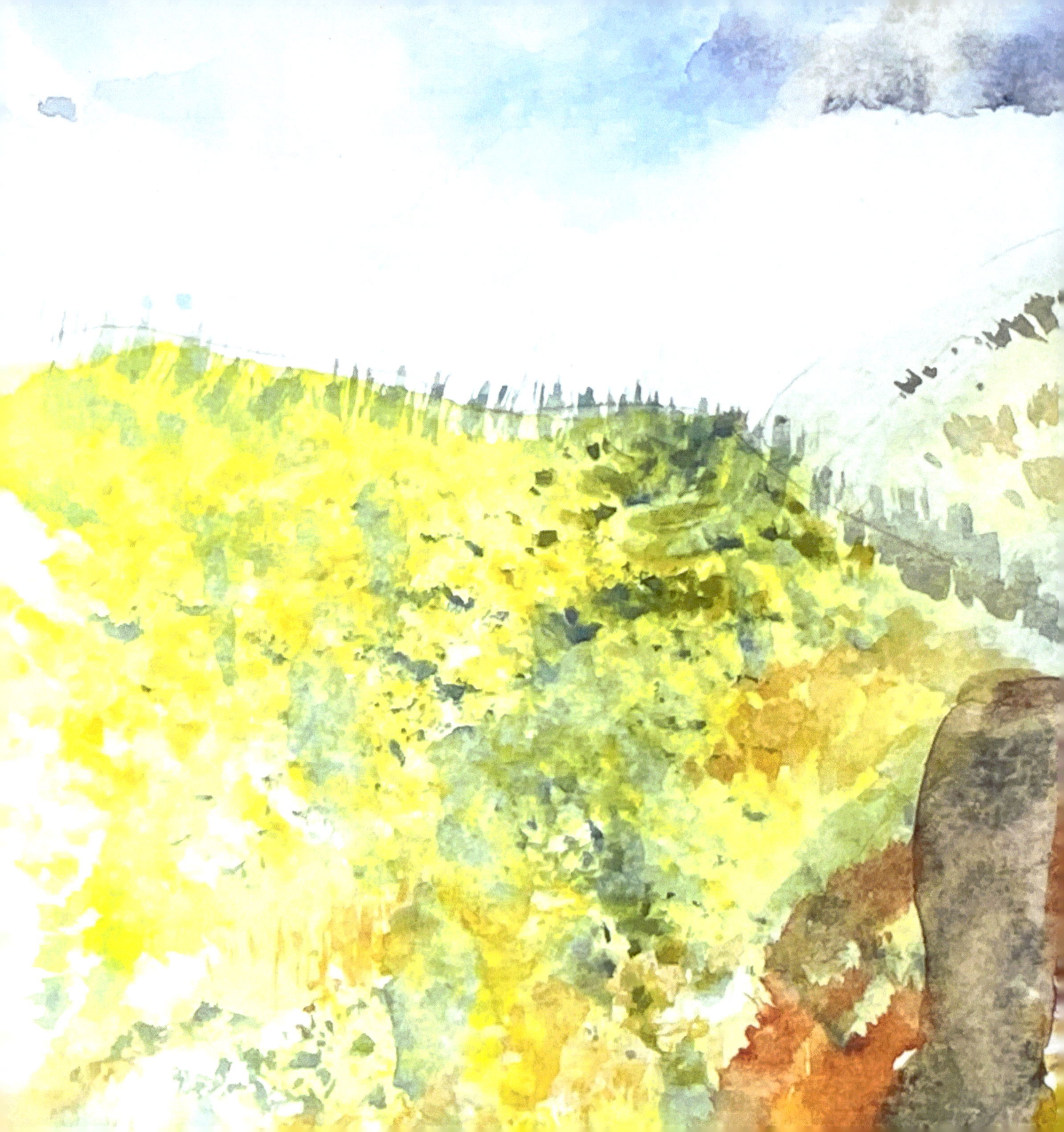

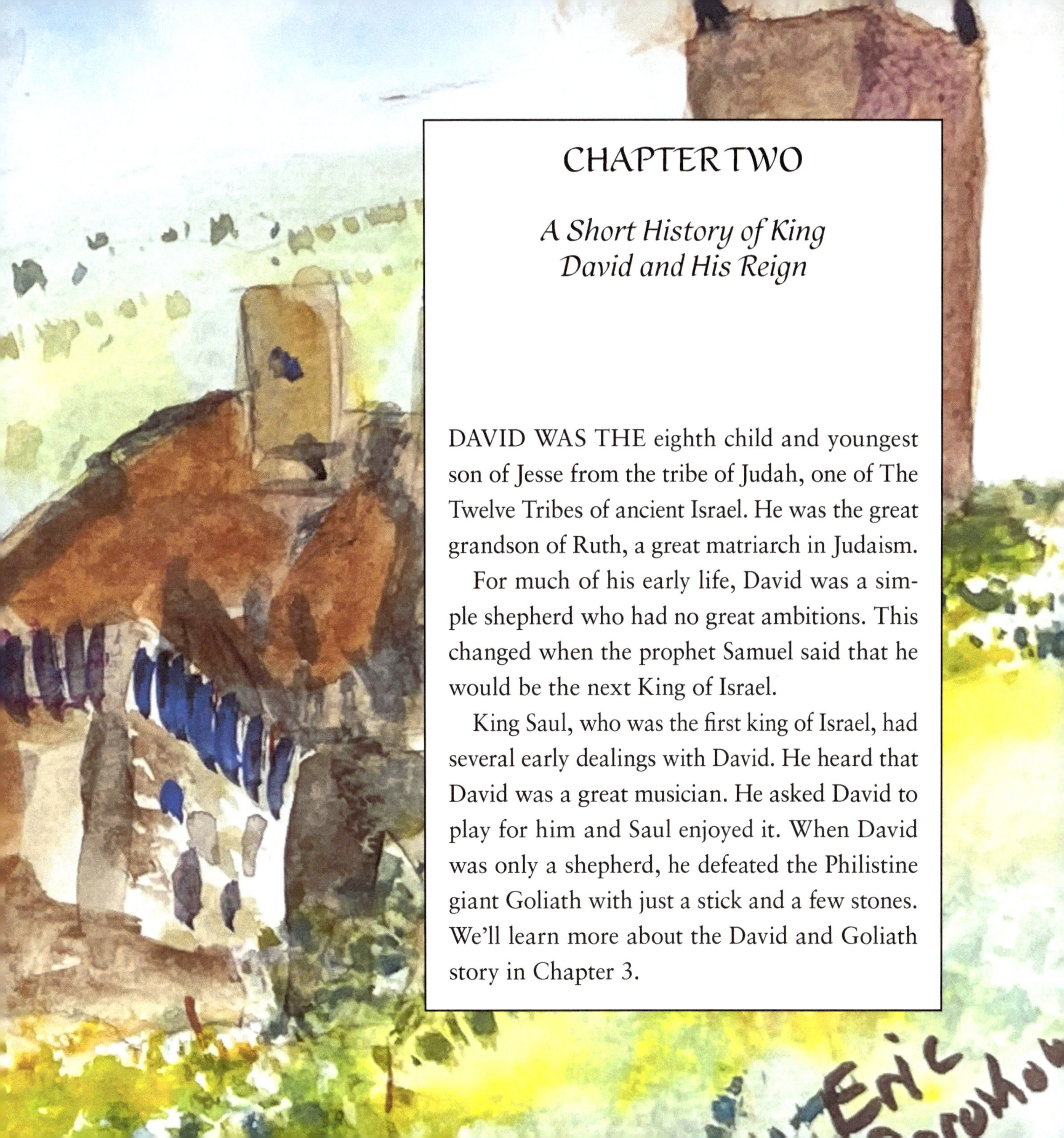

CHAPTER TWO

A Short History of King David and His Reign

DAVID WAS THE eighth child and youngest son of Jesse from the tribe of Judah, one of The Twelve Tribes of ancient Israel. He was the great grandson of Ruth, a great matriarch in Judaism.

For much of his early life, David was a simple shepherd who had no great ambitions. This changed when the prophet Samuel said that he would be the next King of Israel.

King Saul, who was the first king of Israel, had several early dealings with David. He heard that David was a great musician. He asked David to play for him and Saul enjoyed it. When David was only a shepherd, he defeated the Philistine giant Goliath with just a stick and a few stones. We'll learn more about the David and Goliath story in Chapter 3.

David supported the reign of King Saul, who gave David a high rank in his army. He was well liked by his troops and the officers in Saul's army. At first, King Saul liked David, and even permitted David to marry one of his daughters, Micha.

However, as time went along, King Saul became jealous of David, and attempted to have him assassinated.

Saul enlisted his son Jonathan to kill David. However, unbeknownst to Saul, David was friends with Jonathan, who helped David. On one occasion, Jonathan was able to temporarily reverse his father's death decree and convince Saul not to murder David. However, Saul's jealousy continued to overwhelm him, and Saul attempted to kill David a second time. This time, David was tipped off about Saul's intentions from Jonathan and escaped. He eventually found refuge with the King of Moab.

During his flight from Saul, David gained the support of 600 men as he traveled from city to city. At one point, David discovered Saul in a cave and crept up on him. However, instead of killing Saul, he cut a piece of fabric from his coat. David spared his life because he would not go against the dictates of G-d, who had anointed Saul to be King. Despite all of Saul's misdeeds, David considered Saul's life precious and of great value. Although Saul was initially appreciative of David's actions in sparing his life, he continued his pursuit of David.

While trying to avoid capture by Saul, David joined the Philistine King Achish of Gath, who appointed him a general in his army. David raided the cities of nomads who harassed the Jews and gave the spoils to the leaders of the tribe of Judah. The people of Judea were grateful to David and eventually appointed him King of that tribe.

David began a new stage in his life as the King of Judah reigning in Hebron. By that time, Saul and Jonathan had died in a war against the Philistines. Saul's son Ish-Bosheth became the King of Israel. The kingdoms of Judah and Israel fought, with David growing stronger and Saul's son's forces growing weaker.

Eventually, David defeated Saul's son and

Ish-Bosheth was killed. The tribes of Israel were then left without a leader.

They anointed David as their King. He was now the King of both Judah and the remaining eleven tribes. His most important job was to convert the loose confederation of the Twelve Tribes of Israel into one unified political body, and thus he united all Twelve Tribes under his one rule. He was 30 years old at the time. He reigned from 1010-970 BCE, and his reign is often looked on as a golden era.

David's first action while King of the unified Tribes was to capture what is now the City of David in Jerusalem. He fortified it and made it his capital city. He intended the city to be the secular and religious center of all the Tribes of Israel and brought the Holy Ark to that city.

Although David was not permitted to build the first Temple, he prepared for its construction by setting aside materials and giving the building plans to Solomon.

During his reign, David began fighting mostly defensive wars against Israel's neighbors. During these wars, he annexed some land outright.

He also established protectorates over some conquered lands. His successes were achieved both by military power and diplomatic talent. He also took economic considerations into his actions.

Not all the members of the tribes supported the hegemony established by David. For instance, there was agitation from the Tribes of Benjamin and Ephraim against the rule of the House of David.

David's empire extended on both sides of the Jordan River, as far as the Mediterranean Sea. From the capital of Jerusalem, David enforced justice in his empire by establishing professional civil and military administrators. He established twelve administrative districts which were derived from The Twelve Tribes.

David established a strong army, and financed the civil, military, and religious administration of the State based on tribute and taxes collected by district offices. As a result, he was able to take a group of loosely knit tribes and mold them into a national union.

David administered "true justice among all his

people" 2 Samuel 8:15. He treated his subjects fairly and with compassion.

Despite all these accomplishments, David had many challenges and problems during his reign. One famous incident which showed David's dark side occurred while one of his generals, Uriah, was away serving in David's army. David saw the general's wife, Bathsheba, bathing, and became infatuated with her. David then connived a way to have Uriah killed so he could have Bathsheba for himself. He ordered Uriah's comrades to abandon him during the battle, thus easing the way for Uriah to be killed by an opposing army. Following Uriah's death, David took Bathsheba as his wife. When confronted by Nathan the prophet, David saw the evil of his ways, and was wholehearted in his remorse.

G-d severely punished David for his misdeeds. The first child he had with Bathsheba died; however, Bathsheba and David did conceive a second son, Solomon, and he would become David's eventual successor as King. As additional retribution for his misdeeds, David was cursed with the promise of a rebellion from within his own

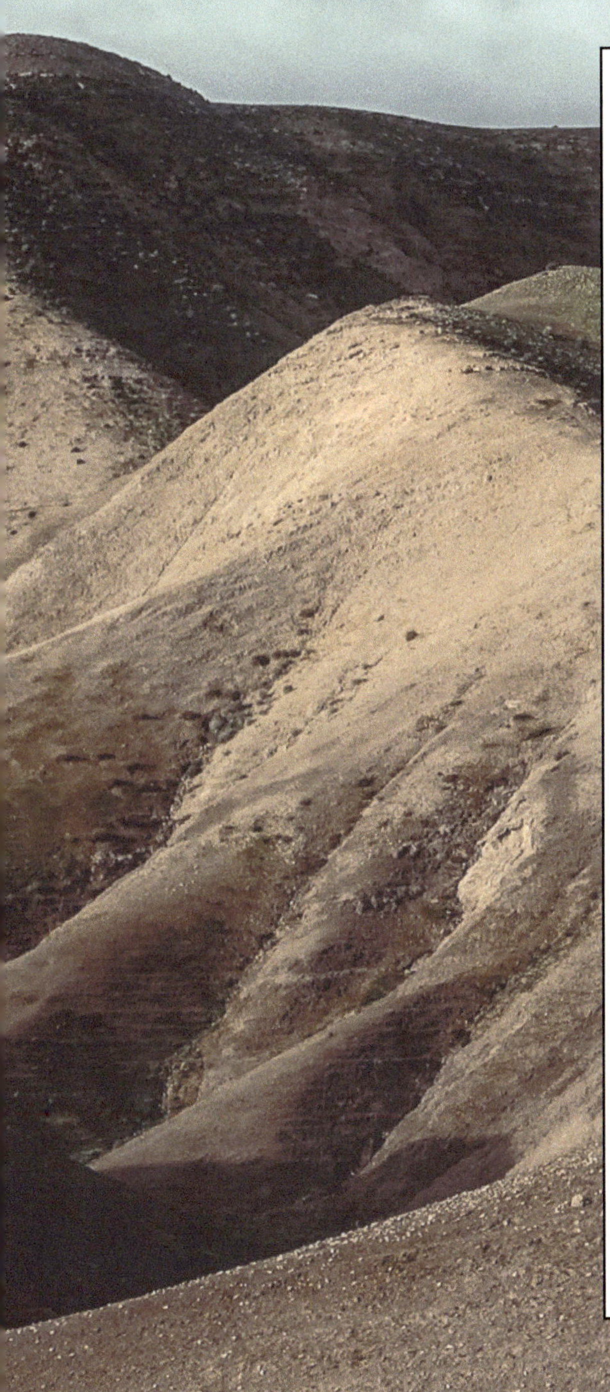

house. As a result, David's family was a cause of personal strife throughout his life.

Examples of this family strife include an incident in which his son Amnon raped Tamar, Amnon's half-sister. Another son, Absalom, killed Amnon. He then led a rebellion against David. David fled Jerusalem and reorganized a counterattack, killing 20,000 of Absalom's Israelite soldiers and Absalom himself. After that, David returned to power.

Another revolt broke out against David's rule when Sheba, from the Tribe of Benjamin, tried to take over power. With the help of loyal subordinates, David succeeded in also defeating that rebellion.

David was able to stop these rebellions and prevent fragmentation of the tribes through the force of his personality, his courage, and his talent of resolving problems with his opponents.

As David grew older, the issue of succession to the throne required resolution. David's oldest son, Adonijah, declared himself King, but David had promised Bathsheba that her son, Solomon, would be king. He publicly anointed

Solomon as his successor. David died after 40 years as king.

Solomon was David's tenth son and the second son of Bathsheba. He became the third and last king of a United Kingdom of Israel. He built the Temple to house the Ark of the Covenant per the wishes of King David and G-d. Solomon was renowned for his wisdom, his writings, and his building accomplishments. Soon after he died, there was a civil war among the Tribes. This was the end of the United Kingdom of Israel that David had worked so hard to establish.

Many Rabbis believe that David wrote, or at least edited, the Book of Psalms. As we shall see, the Davidic Psalms are filled with lessons, inspiration, and courage, even for us today.

In addition to all his accomplishments, David was a skillful musician and a great poet. The authors of *The Encyclopedia Judaica* summarize the life of David by writing that he was a real character, with all aspects depicted. "At times his strengths were manifested, and at times his weaknesses. As King of all the tribes of Israel and ruler of a great and extensive kingdom, he

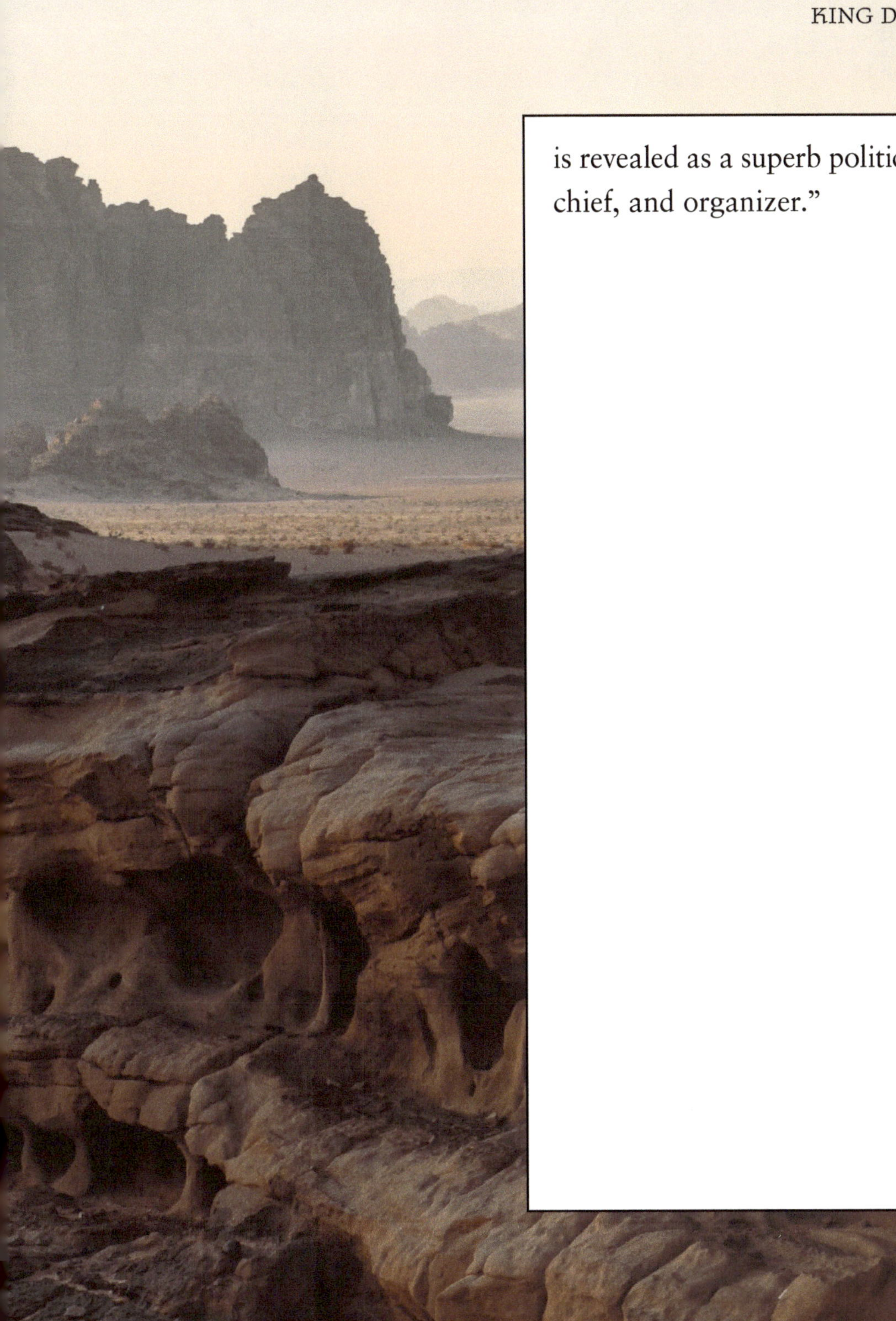

is revealed as a superb politician, commander in chief, and organizer."

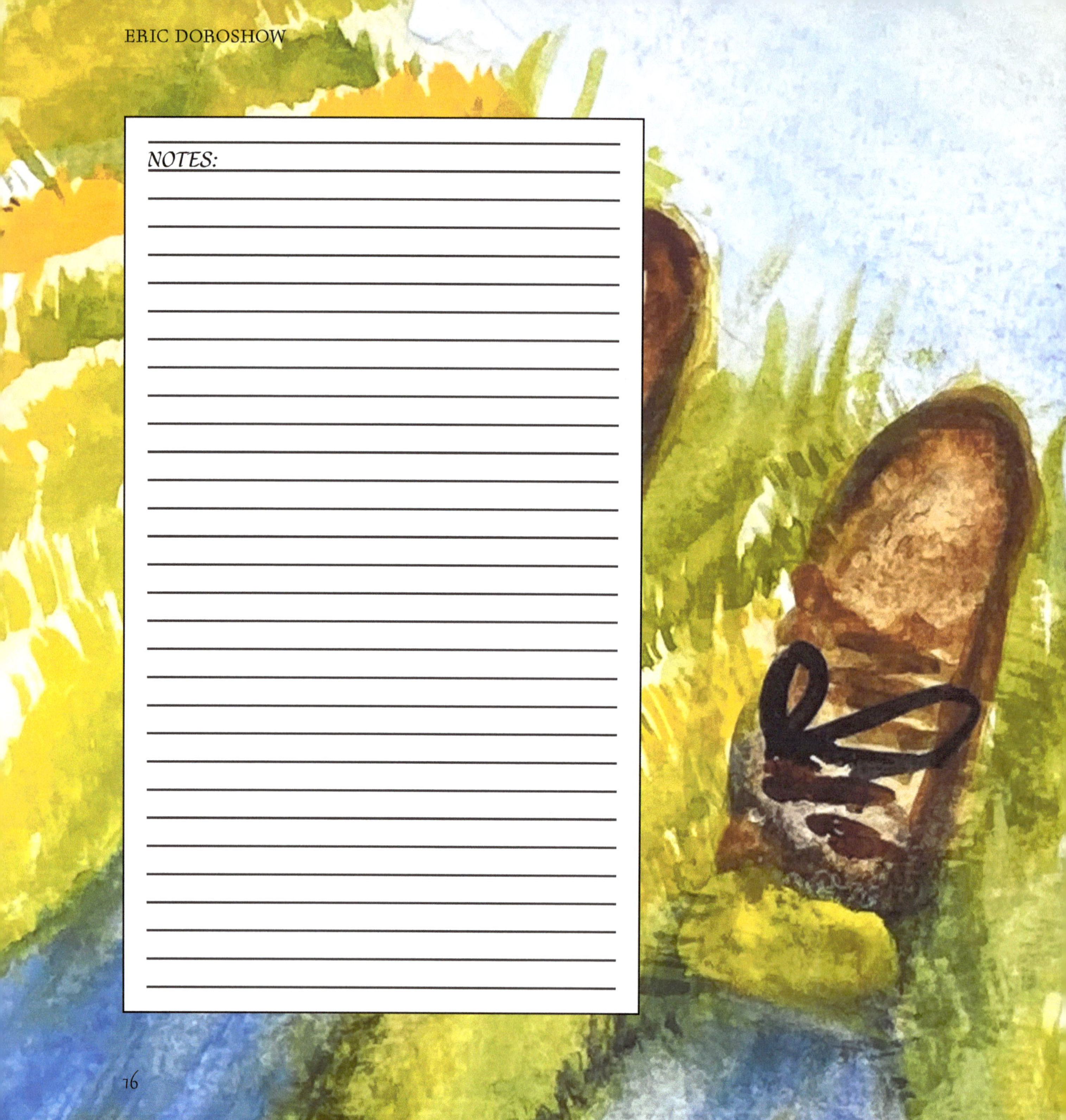

NOTES:

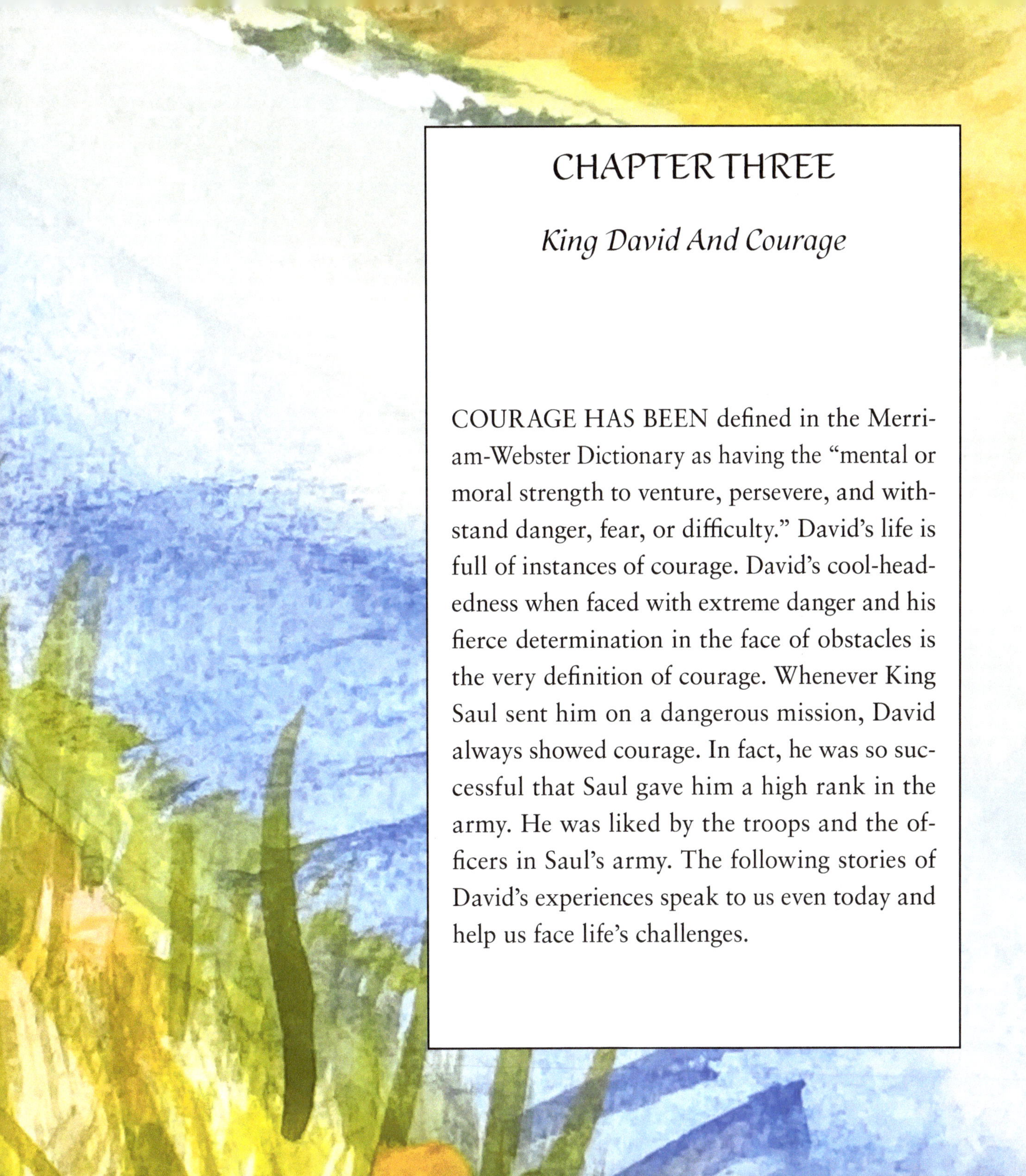

CHAPTER THREE

King David And Courage

COURAGE HAS BEEN defined in the Merriam-Webster Dictionary as having the "mental or moral strength to venture, persevere, and withstand danger, fear, or difficulty." David's life is full of instances of courage. David's cool-headedness when faced with extreme danger and his fierce determination in the face of obstacles is the very definition of courage. Whenever King Saul sent him on a dangerous mission, David always showed courage. In fact, he was so successful that Saul gave him a high rank in the army. He was liked by the troops and the officers in Saul's army. The following stories of David's experiences speak to us even today and help us face life's challenges.

David and Goliath

One of the first instances in which David showed courage is the well-known story of David fighting Goliath. David was a shepherd, inexperienced in warfare, but that didn't stop him from going up against a feared opponent.

The Philistines were enemies of King Saul of the Israelites. The Philistines assembled their forces for battle against the army of King Saul. A champion of the Philistine force, named Goliath, challenged the Israelites to a one-on-one battle to settle the results of the war. Saul and the Israelites were dismayed and were terror-stricken. Skilled warriors cowered in fear. Yet David accepted the challenge to face off against Goliath.

As told in I Samuel 17:33-37, Saul said that David could not fight Goliath. He was only a boy, whereas Goliath was a warrior. Yet David reminded Saul that while a shepherd, he killed both lion and bear. He trusted that the Lord would protect him.

David took no sword, only a few stones in his

pocket and a sling in his hand. When Goliath saw him, he taunted David, threatening to "give your flesh to the birds of the sky, and the beasts of the field" I Samuel 17:43. David showed immense courage by standing his ground, calmly taking a stone out of his bag, putting it in his slingshot, and hitting Goliath in the forehead. Goliath fell face down on the ground, then David pulled out Goliath's large sword from its sheath and cut off his head.

David Confronts Saul

As we have seen in Chapter 2, Saul became jealous of David's popularity. As a result, David fled and traveled from city to city with the support of 600 men. At a place called Ein Gedi, he crept up on Saul while he was in a cave. David could have easily killed Saul. Instead, he showed great courage by stealthily cutting a piece of his cloak and confronting him. He used the occasion to tell Saul that he could have killed him, yet he did not. He told Saul that he had done nothing evil or rebellious. Saul admitted that he had treated David badly, then broke down and admitted that

David would be King one day. He asked David to swear that he would not destroy Saul's descendants when he became King. David agreed.

The Bathsheba Affair

Bathsheba was the wife of Uriah, one of David's warriors. One day, while his men were at war, David saw Bathsheba from his rooftop. He became infatuated with her and ordered her brought to see him. He then began an affair with her. Soon thereafter, he got Bathsheba pregnant and pretended that Uriah was the father. He then sent Uriah to the front lines of battle where he was killed. After that, David married Bathsheba.

In II Samuel 12, it is written that the Lord was displeased with what David had done. He sent Nathan the Prophet to speak to him. When confronted by Nathan, David saw the evil of his ways and was wholehearted in his remorse.

A line from the Psalm 51:17 shows how David pleaded for forgiveness when he stated, "O Lord, You shall open my lips, and my mouth will recite Your praise." David could easily have thrown out Nathan or even killed him. He did not. These actions showed David's courage in understanding what he had done wrong, accepting responsibility for his actions, and asking for full forgiveness: "I have sinned against the Lord" II Samuel 12:13.

King David Destroys the Amalekites

THE ISRAELITE BATTLES AGAINST THE AMALEKITES BEFORE KING DAVID

According to *The Encyclopedia Judaica*, the Amalekites lived in the Negev desert and adjoining deserts in what is known today as southern Israel.

The Amalekites were a hereditary enemy of Israel from the wilderness times until the time of David. Amalek was the first enemy that Israel encountered when it crossed the Sea of Reeds. Some Rabbis believe that whenever Israel begins to doubt G-d, Amalek unexpectedly assails them.

In the Bible, there are numerous stories of battles between the Israelites and Amalekites. As told in Exodus 17:16, Amalek attacked Israel

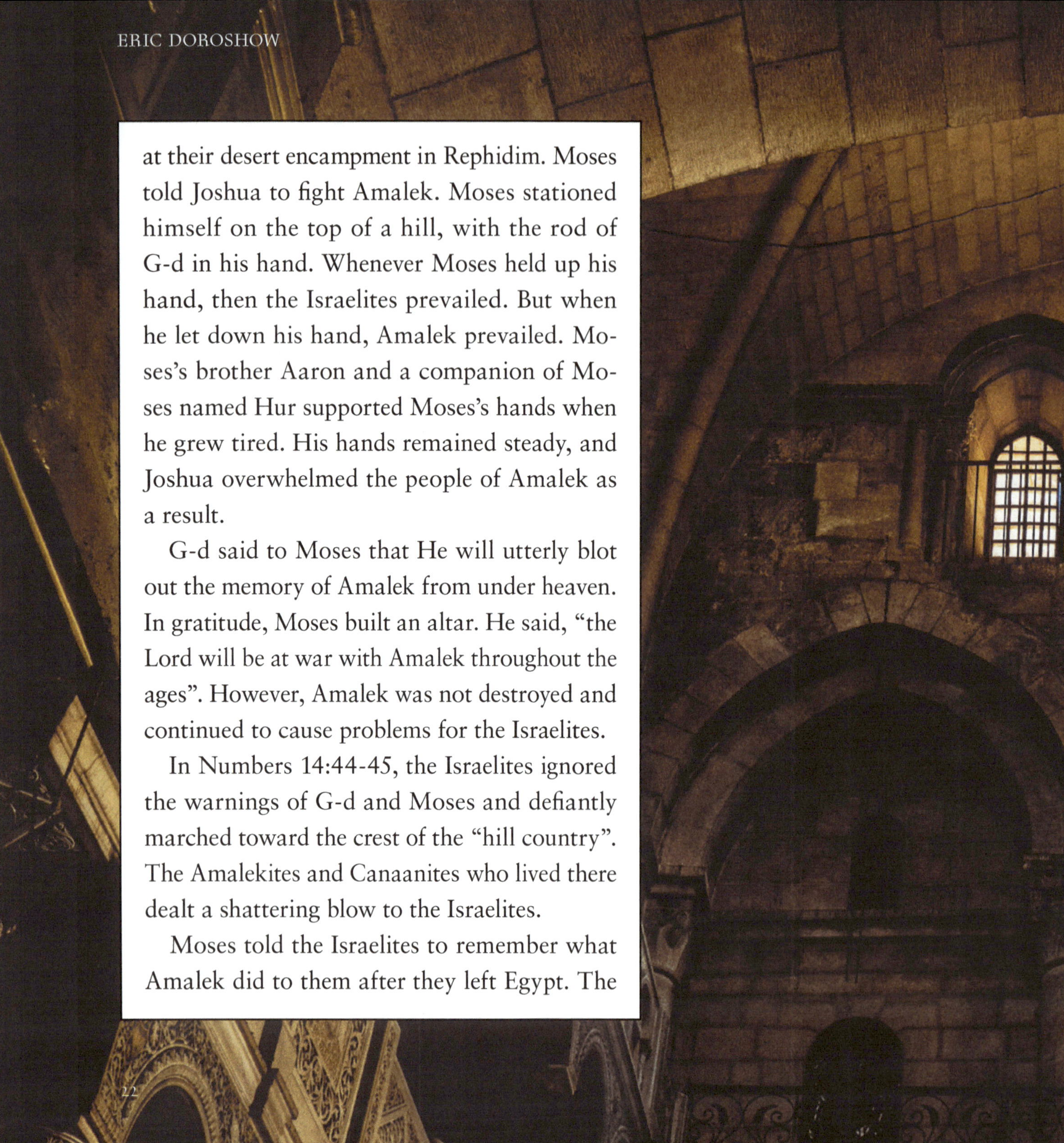

at their desert encampment in Rephidim. Moses told Joshua to fight Amalek. Moses stationed himself on the top of a hill, with the rod of G-d in his hand. Whenever Moses held up his hand, then the Israelites prevailed. But when he let down his hand, Amalek prevailed. Moses's brother Aaron and a companion of Moses named Hur supported Moses's hands when he grew tired. His hands remained steady, and Joshua overwhelmed the people of Amalek as a result.

G-d said to Moses that He will utterly blot out the memory of Amalek from under heaven. In gratitude, Moses built an altar. He said, "the Lord will be at war with Amalek throughout the ages". However, Amalek was not destroyed and continued to cause problems for the Israelites.

In Numbers 14:44-45, the Israelites ignored the warnings of G-d and Moses and defiantly marched toward the crest of the "hill country". The Amalekites and Canaanites who lived there dealt a shattering blow to the Israelites.

Moses told the Israelites to remember what Amalek did to them after they left Egypt. The

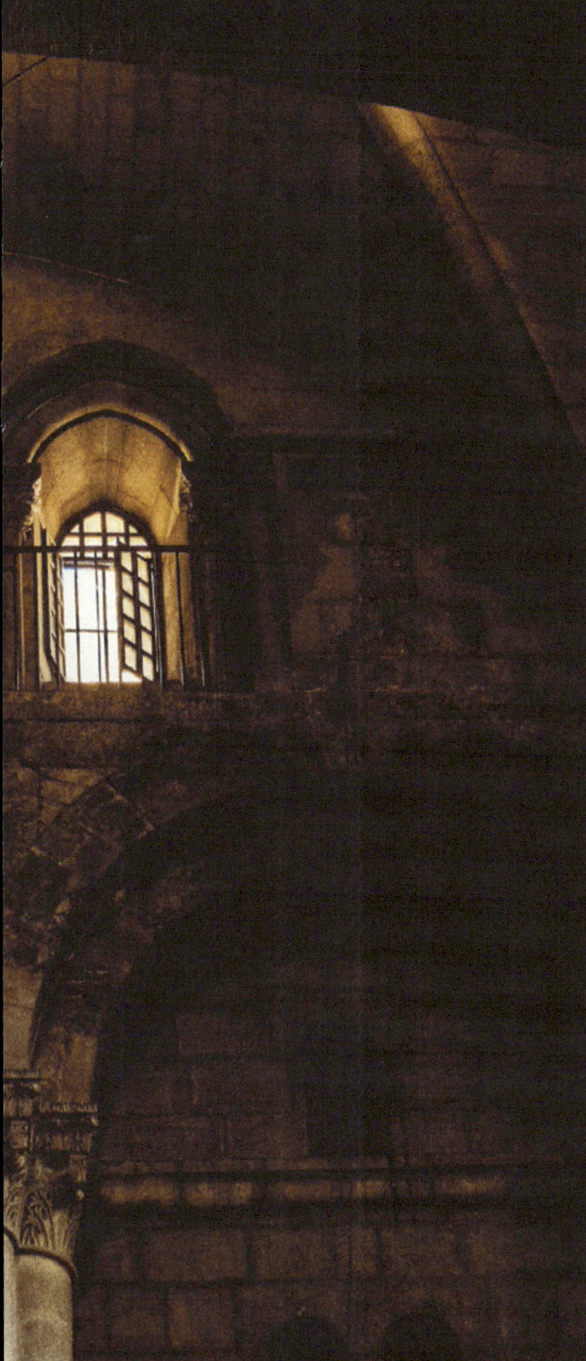

Amalekites were undeterred by fear of G-d and surprised the Israelites on their journey. When they were hungry and tired, the Amalekites killed all the stragglers in the rear. The Israelites were told by the Lord to "blot out the memory of Amalek from under heaven. Do not forget!" Deuteronomy 25:17.

During the period of the Judges, which post-dated the settlement in ancient Israel by The Twelve Tribes, the Amalekites participated with other nations in attacking the Israelite tribes. They joined the people of Moab and captured the "city of palms" Judges 3:12-13. This city is now believed to be Jericho.

The struggles against the Amalekites continued into King Saul's reign. A war began began because of a commandment of the Lord to King Saul to smite them, I Samuel 15. Saul was victorious and captured King Agag of Amalek alive. Saul killed all the inhabitants but, contrary to the edict of G-d, spared the choicest sheep and oxen for sacrificing. As a result of Saul's defiance of the Lord's will, the Lord rejected Saul as a King.

The Amalekites were never destroyed by Saul. At the end of his reign, they were still causing havoc by their raids in the Negev desert.

KING DAVID ELIMINATES THE AMALEKITE THREAT

When David became King, one of his primary goals was to eliminate the Amalekite threat. During his reign, the Amalekites raided and destroyed a town in the tribe of Judea called Ziklag. David and his men arrived at Ziklag and found that the Amalekites had burned the town down and had taken the women and children into captivity. David's two wives were among those captured. David was in great danger, not only from the Amalekites, but also from his own troops. They were embittered by the destruction of the town and abduction of the people. David sought strength from the Lord and inquired if he should pursue the raiders. The Lord said, "Pursue, for you shall overtake and you shall rescue" I Samuel 30:8.

David took six hundred men to pursue the invaders, but 200 were too ill to continue. Thus

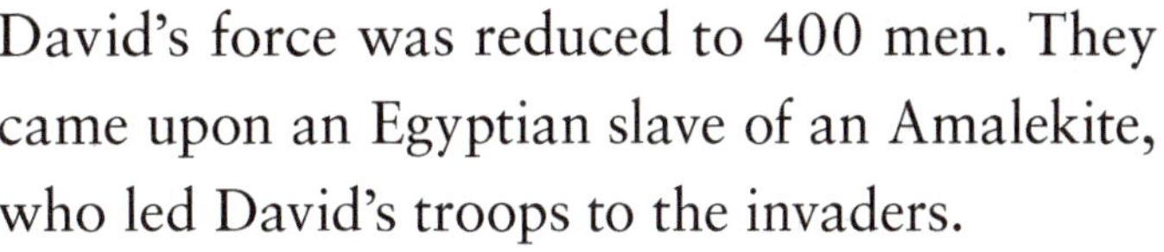

David's force was reduced to 400 men. They came upon an Egyptian slave of an Amalekite, who led David's troops to the invaders.

Showing great courage, David and his men attacked them before dawn and into the evening of the next day. He rescued the people, the items the Amalekites had taken, and his two wives.

David showed a keen sense of justice by distributing the spoils from his victory over the Amalekites equally between the soldiers who fought and to those too ill to fight. He also shared his spoils with the elders of the Tribe of Judah.

David was therefore successful in resisting the long-standing Amalekite threat. Before David became King, they captured the Holy Ark of the Israelites.

King David and the Philistines

The Philistines were a people of Aegean origin who were often at war with the Israelites. Beginning long before the time of King David, the Philistines were a great threat to the Israelites. For instance, during the exodus from Egypt, the Israelites took a southern route to circumvent them.

As we have read in the David and Goliath story in Chapter 3, Goliath was a Philistine. The Bible tells us that King Saul was so impressed by David's courage in standing up to Goliath, that he permitted him to marry his daughter, Michal, upon payment of an odd price: 100 foreskins of the Philistines. Saul eventually enlisted him to the rank of captain in his army. With great courage, David continued to have successes in battle against the Philistines as a captain in Saul's army.

However, as we have seen in Chapter 2, Saul grew afraid of David. It appears David's popularity with the Israelites, as well as Saul's jealousy, were the driving factors in his fears. As a result, David became Saul's enemy. When David found out about Saul's intent to kill him, he fled.

One battle against the Philistines occurred even while David was a fugitive from King Saul. The Judean town of Keilah was brutally plundered by Philistines. David felt that he had to stop these Philistine incursions. David consulted the Lord, who urged him to attack the Philistines and save Keilah. David's men were

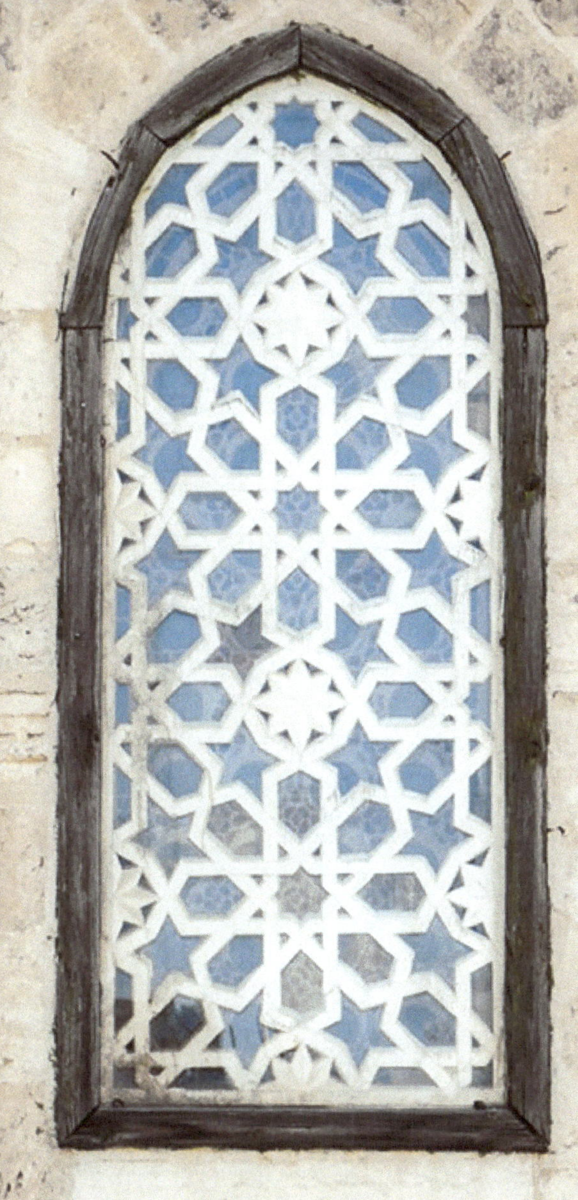

afraid. Demonstrating great courage, David rallied his troops and led his forces into battle with a well-armed foe. He inflicted a severe defeat on the Philistines.

Ironically, while David was fleeing from King Saul, he found refuge with the Philistines. David and 600 of his followers entered the service of Achish, a Philistine King. He was given the city of Ziklag in which to live, and the Philistines hoped he would raid the Israelites from that city. However, David was careful to raid only the nomads who harassed the Israelites and not the Israelites themselves.

When King Achish was mustering his forces for a battle against King Saul and the Israelites, David and his men were in the last unit. However, the Philistine army officers were angry about this and rejected David's help.

Thereafter, the Philistines attacked King Saul without David's help. The Philistines were victorious, killing both Saul and his son Jonathan, who had become David's friend. After this event, David was anointed as King over Israel.

According to the Jewish Virtual Library:

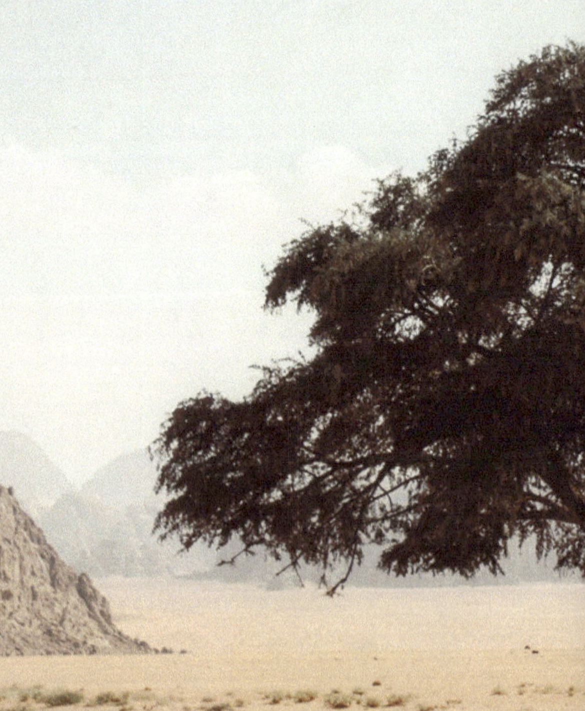

David's first action as king was to capture what is now the City of David in Jerusalem, fortify it and build himself a palace. When the Philistines heard that David had been anointed king and was threatening their hegemony, they attacked, spread out over the Valley of Raphaim and captured Bethlehem. David retaliated and, in three battles, forced the Philistines out of Israel.

Once David had established the safety of his kingdom, he brought the Holy Ark, which had been passed from city to city, to Jerusalem. He then wanted to build a temple to G-d and consulted Nathan the prophet. Natan replied to David that G-d would always be with David, but it would be up to David's son to build the Temple because David had been a warrior and shed blood.

David's Final Words to Solomon

Not only was David courageous, but he also passed on advice about courage to his successor, Solomon. When David was dying, he assembled his sons and spoke to them his last words of guidance and admonition. One of David's most eloquent comments on courage comes from 1 Chronicles 28:20 when he said to his son Solomon, "Be strong and of good courage and do it; do not fear and be not dismayed, for the Lord G-d, my G-d, is with you..."

NOTES:

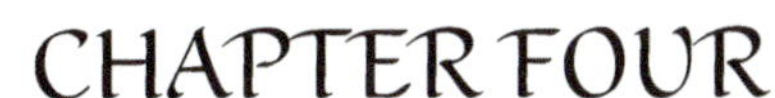

CHAPTER FOUR

King David And Christianity

DAVID PLAYS AN important part in the Christian religion. Christians believe that King David was the ideal man, the ideal King. According to the apostle Peter, David was also a prophet. He believed that Jesus descended from the lineage of David, and that Jesus fulfilled his kingship, Acts 2:25-36. Peter quoted Psalms 16:8-11 and 110:1 as prophecies of David about the coming of the Messiah.

Additionally, there is additional material in the New Testament's gospels of the lineage between David and Jesus. There were two distinct genealogies of Jesus in the Gospels of Matthew and Luke. In Matthew 1:1-7 and Luke 3:23-28 it is written that the ancestry of Christ was descended directly from David. Jesus' Davidic ancestry was also mentioned by Paul in Romans 15.

Shepherd analogies often appear in the writings of Christian religion. In the Old and New Testaments, G-d is frequently called the shepherd of his people. David was also a shepherd. In Ezekiel 34, the prophet utters G-d's promise that He will give his people a shepherd in the Davidic line who will lead them to salvation from false rulers. In the 10th Chapter of John, Jesus is portrayed as a "good shepherd" who cares for the sheep. The shepherd is considered by many to be the messianic figure of Jesus.

Some Christian authors considered David to be a type of Jesus. Others considered him a prophet. In medieval times, he was regarded as an exemplary knight. The Church regarded David as the prototype of a king obeying the Church's precepts. During the Middle Ages, the anointment of David as King by Samuel was often used by the Church as a basis for the anointment of kings and emperors.

The Greek historian of Christianity, Eusebius, lived during the first century AD after the capture of Jerusalem by the Roman emperor Vespasian. According to him, Vespasian ordered a

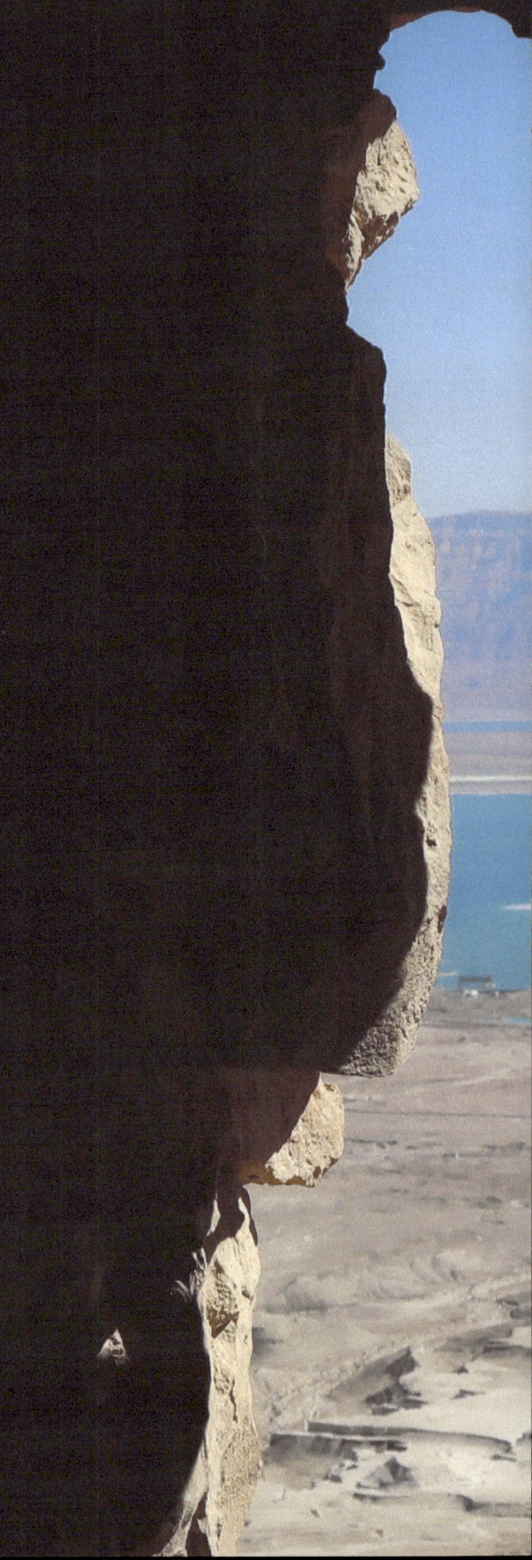

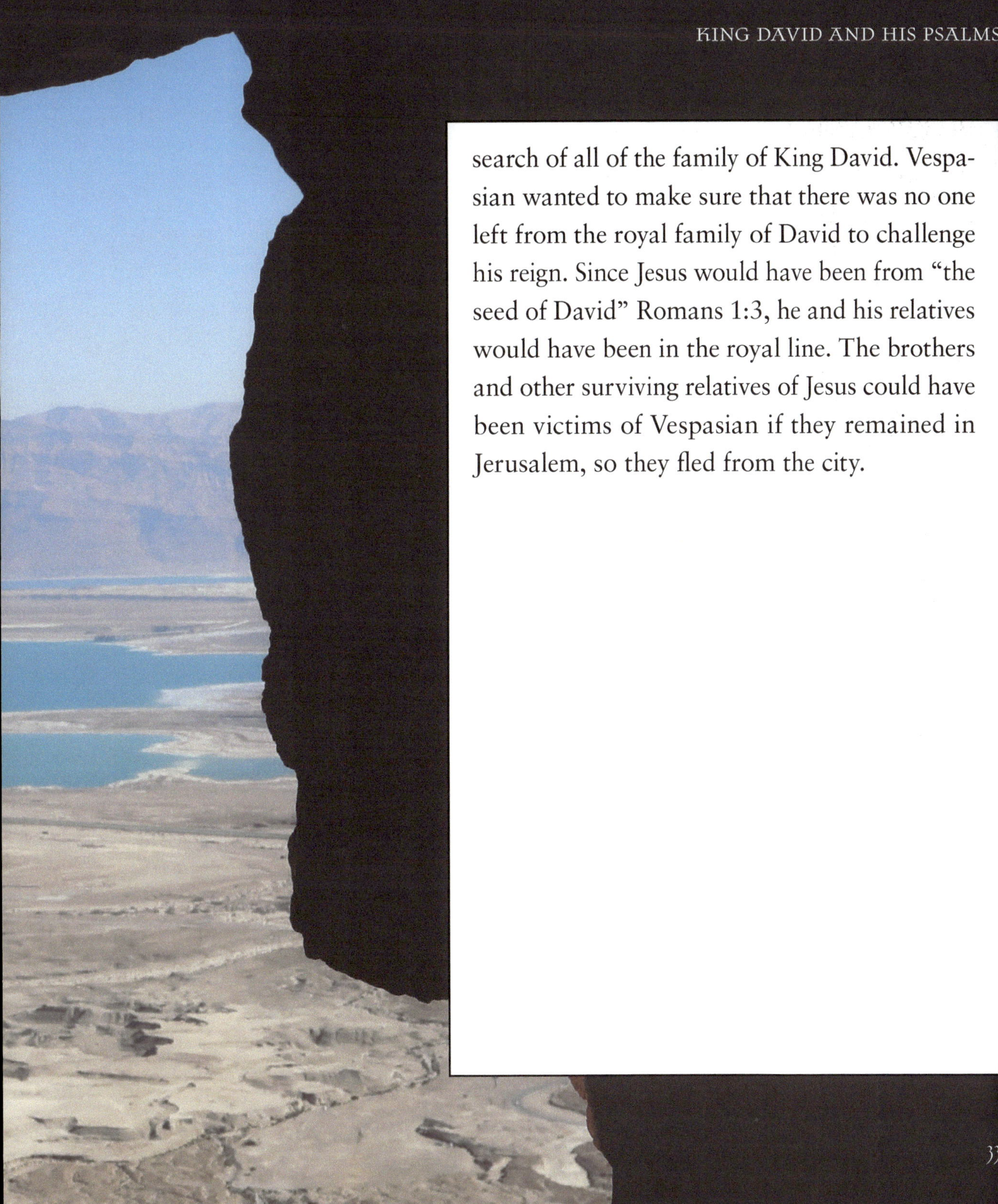

search of all of the family of King David. Vespasian wanted to make sure that there was no one left from the royal family of David to challenge his reign. Since Jesus would have been from "the seed of David" Romans 1:3, he and his relatives would have been in the royal line. The brothers and other surviving relatives of Jesus could have been victims of Vespasian if they remained in Jerusalem, so they fled from the city.

NOTES:

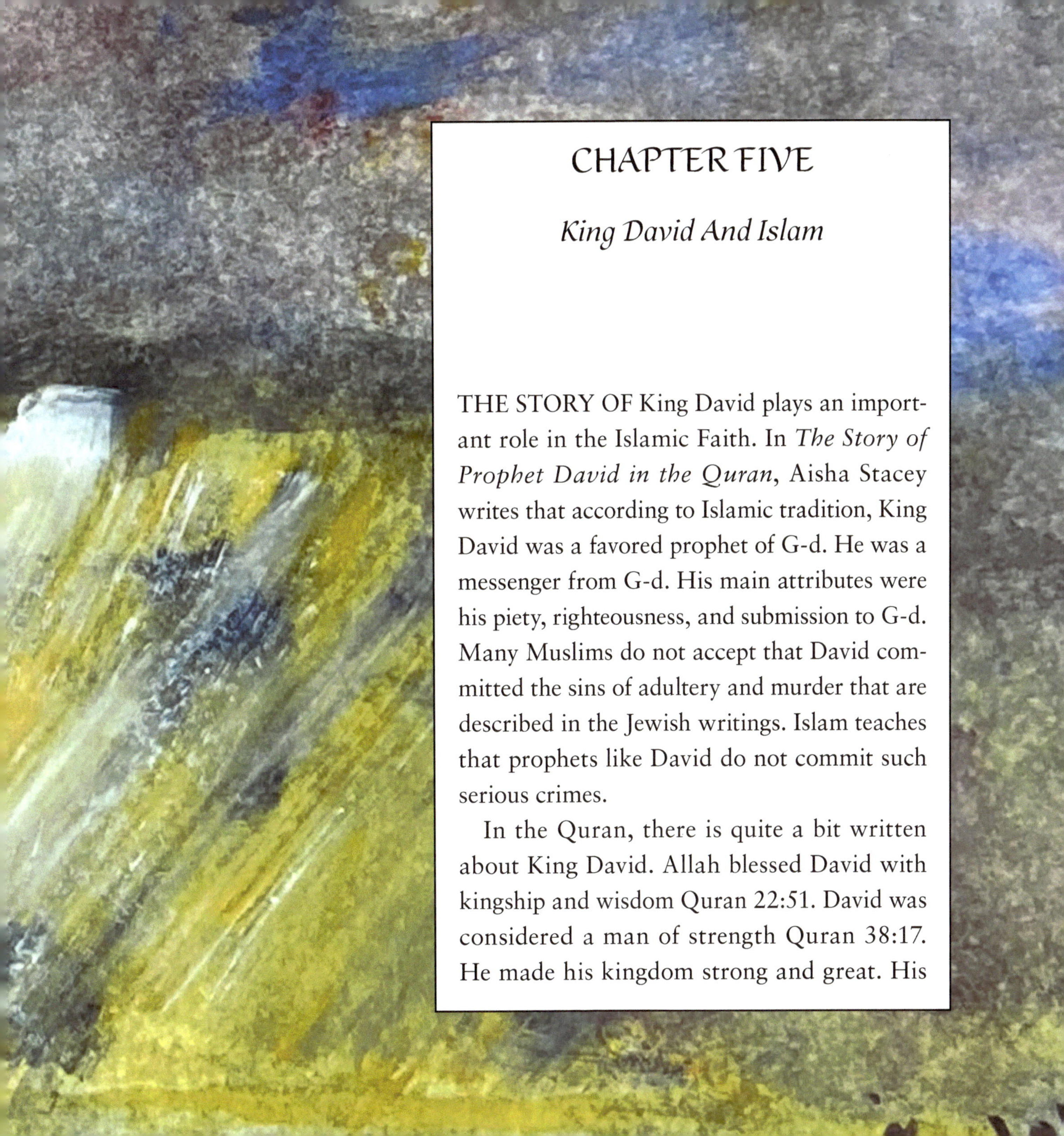

CHAPTER FIVE

King David And Islam

THE STORY OF King David plays an important role in the Islamic Faith. In *The Story of Prophet David in the Quran*, Aisha Stacey writes that according to Islamic tradition, King David was a favored prophet of G-d. He was a messenger from G-d. His main attributes were his piety, righteousness, and submission to G-d. Many Muslims do not accept that David committed the sins of adultery and murder that are described in the Jewish writings. Islam teaches that prophets like David do not commit such serious crimes.

In the Quran, there is quite a bit written about King David. Allah blessed David with kingship and wisdom Quran 22:51. David was considered a man of strength Quran 38:17. He made his kingdom strong and great. His enemies feared him without engaging in war with him. He centralized power, developed a significant military organization, and made his capital in Jerusalem. G-d gave him wisdom and sound judgment in speech and decision Quran 38:18-20. In 34:10, it was written that mountains echo his hymns, and the birds as well. Iron was made moldable for him. He used his beautiful voice to delight people and remind them of G-d.

In his book *The Stories of the Prophets*, Hafiz Ibn Kathir writes that during the battle with Goliath, many soldiers lost their faith in Allah. Allah tested them, and David was among the very few who proved that their belief was strong and unwavering. Allah gave permission to David to kill Goliath; after killing him, Allah gave David the kingship and gift of prophethood Quran 2:251.

David's humbleness was first shown when he did not brag about his fame; rather, he sang G-d's praises while in the desert. As a result of his sincerity and the sweetness of his voice, he was endowed with the faculty of understanding the languages of birds and animals. Plants, birds, beasts, and even mountains responded to his voice glorifying Allah.

Being very pious, David divided his day into four parts. In part one, he earned his living and rested. In the second, he listened to the complaints of his subjects. In the third, he preached sermons, and in the final part he spent time praising G-d and praying. David would also fast every other day, thereby showing his piety.

In her article, "The Story of Prophet David in the Quran", Aisha Stacey describes "the account of the litigants." One day, two brothers climbed over the wall in David's prayer palace and asked David to judge their claims. They were 2 angels sent by G-d to test David. One brother had 99 ewes (sheep) and wanted the only ewe his brother possessed. David, in error, first ruled in favor of the poorer brother who had only one ewe. He ruled without hearing all the evidence, and was biased in favor of the poorer brother. He suddenly realized this was a test from G-d and that he made a terrible mistake. He bowed his head and asked for forgiveness. David passed the test, and G-d made David a vicegerent of the earth to judge truth among men.

In recognition of his exalted status, David received the Psalms Quran 17:55. The Book of David in Islam is called the Zabur. The Psalms are believed to have been somewhat corrupted over time. Some believe that the original message is now gone; however, Islam teaches that the Psalms still deserve great respect.

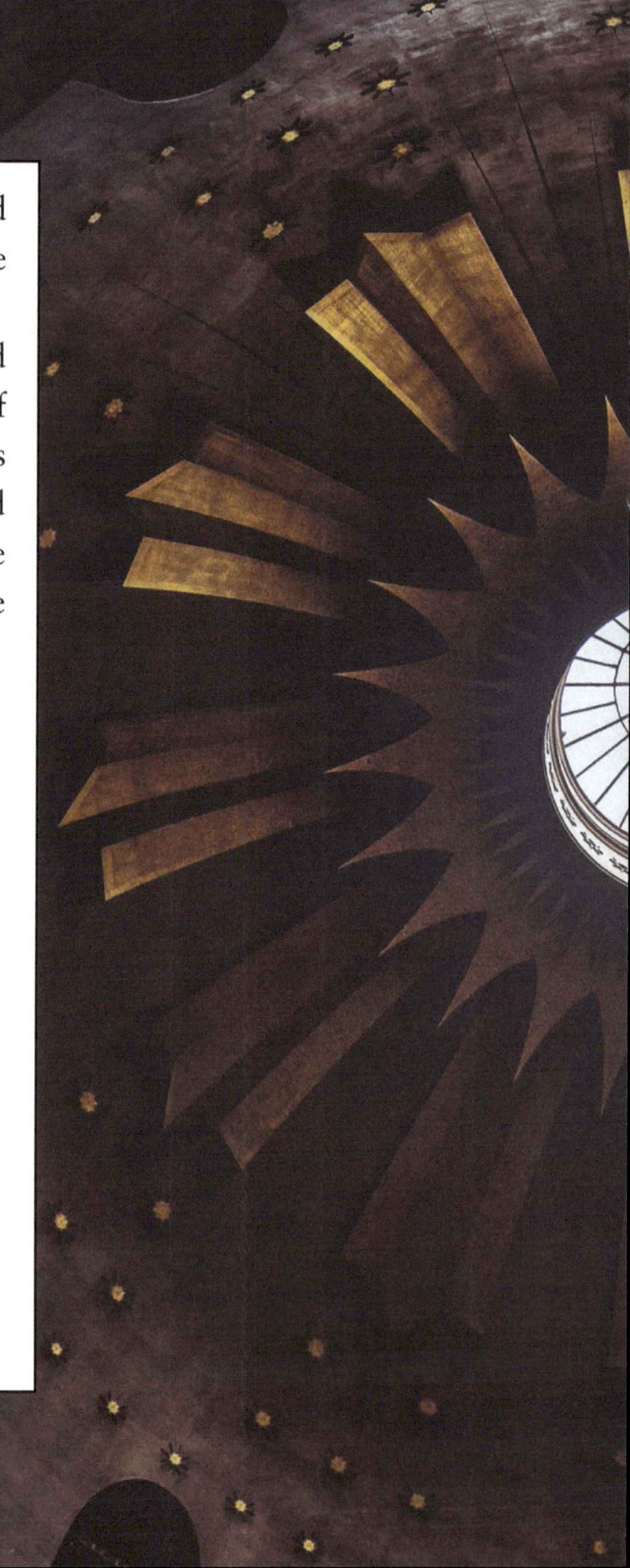

NOTES:

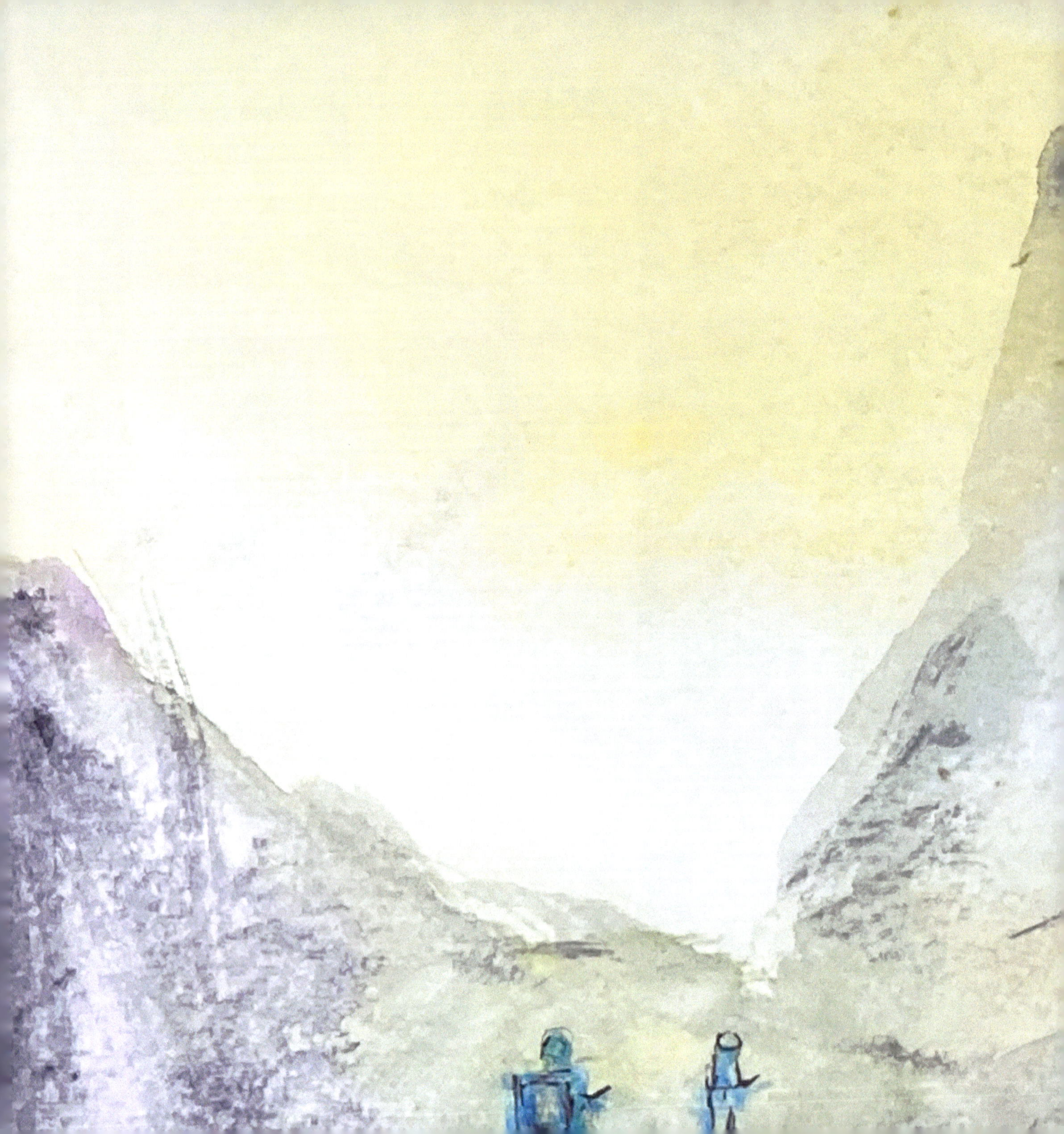

CHAPTER SIX

King David And Judaism

THE STORY OF KING DAVID is fundamental and foundational in Judaism. For many modern Jews, the story of David in the Bible has two aspects. First is the Messianic concept. The Messiah who will build the third temple will be from the Davidic dynasty. He will be sent by G-d to usher in a new golden age. Second is the historical concept. King David, even with all his faults, was a righteous King and a noble servant of G-d. He united The Twelve Tribes of Israel into a strong nation and his decisions were just and equitable.

In *The Encyclopedia Judaica*, the authors identify three stages in the Biblical history of King David and Messianism. In Stage I, the doctrine appears that the Lord has chosen David and his descendants to reign over Israel forever.

David's power will endure not only through his lifetime, but will also be inherited by an endless chain of his successors. In Stage II, David's empire had collapsed after the death of Solomon. During this stage, there was hope that the descendants of David would reign over a united Judea and Israel. A united nation will also have influence on other neighboring countries. In Stage III, the prophet Isaiah emphasized the attributes of the future King of a united Israel and Judea. His reign will be just and charismatic.

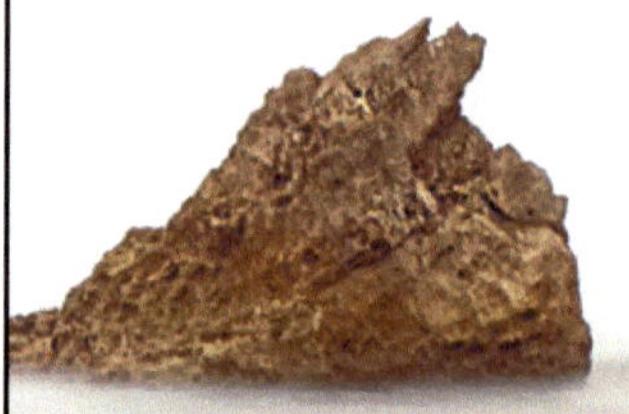

Many Orthodox Jews believe that the Messiah will be a scion of the House of David. He will reign in Jerusalem and will rebuild the Temple. For many Reform Jews, their version of the Messiah is much different. They believe that the Messianic age portends a perfect world, just around the corner. Jews will be the brave carriers of a universalist message of justice to be heeded by all nations.

Today, Jews pray daily for the coming of the Messiah. For example, the silent prayer called the Amidah states: "May our remembrance rise, come and be accepted before Thee, with

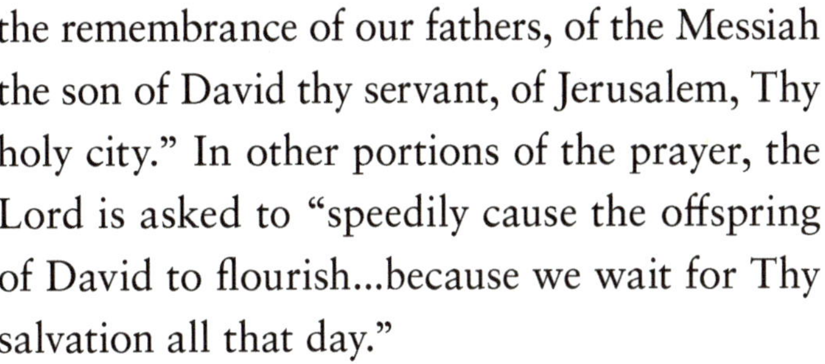

the remembrance of our fathers, of the Messiah the son of David thy servant, of Jerusalem, Thy holy city." In other portions of the prayer, the Lord is asked to "speedily cause the offspring of David to flourish...because we wait for Thy salvation all that day."

In other parts of the service, well known stories about King David's life are recited. For instance, several Psalms of David are recited to show David's courage and inspiration. The stories of David's devotion to the Lord are also recited.

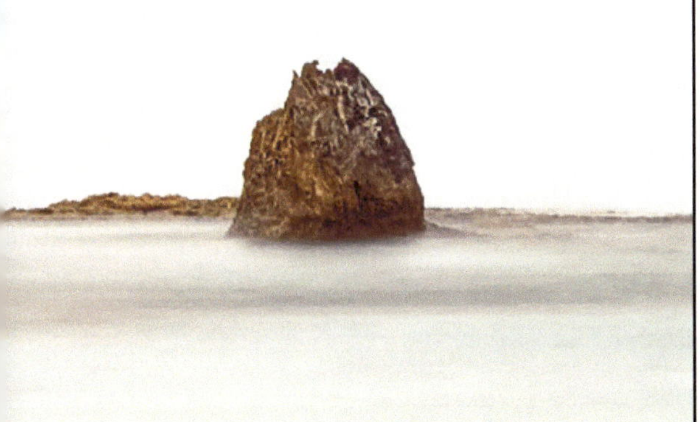

The Ashrei is a prayer recited at least three times a day, and is an important part of the Jewish liturgy. The prayer is composed primarily of Davidic Psalm 145. That Psalm is an alphabetic poem of 21 verses. Except for one verse, each verse begins with a different letter of the Hebrew alphabet, arranged alphabetically. The prayer is about three major concepts. First: people are happy when they are close to G-d. Second: G-d cares about all humans, including the poor and oppressed. Third: G-d rewards good behavior and evil is punished. The Talmud, which is a body of Jewish civil and ceremonial law and legend, states that anyone who recites the Ashrei three times a day is assured of life in the world to come Ber. 4b. We'll learn more about Psalm 145 in Chapter 9.

David's image among Rabbis is multifaceted according to *The Encyclopedia Judaica*. First, they believe that the sovereignty of David shall never lapse. G-d looks forward to David being King until the end of generations. Second, David's physical strength is praised. David waged eighteen battles: three for his own benefit and fifteen for the benefit of Israel. When he went to war, he made himself hard as steel. Third, David was venerated as a great poet who composed the Psalms. In Chapter 9, we'll discuss in detail 9 of King David's Psalms. Fourth, David was a great scholar. He was a great authority of Jewish law and he did not cease learning. Finally, he was considered a great musician: the sweet singer of the songs of Israel II Samuel 23. In 1 Samuel 16:23, it is written that whenever Saul was in a bad mood "David would take to the lyre and play it. Saul would find relief and feel

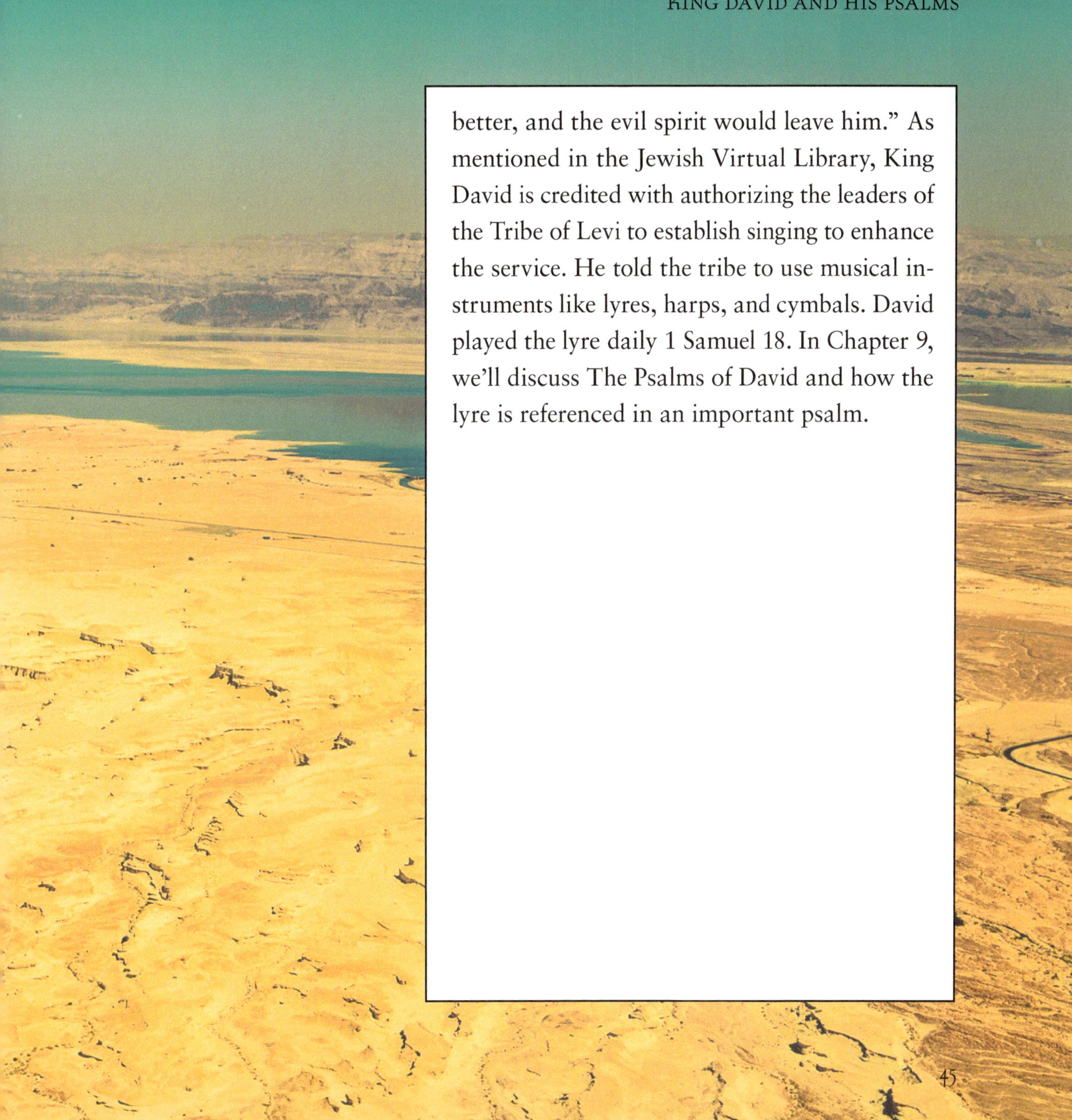

better, and the evil spirit would leave him." As mentioned in the Jewish Virtual Library, King David is credited with authorizing the leaders of the Tribe of Levi to establish singing to enhance the service. He told the tribe to use musical instruments like lyres, harps, and cymbals. David played the lyre daily 1 Samuel 18. In Chapter 9, we'll discuss The Psalms of David and how the lyre is referenced in an important psalm.

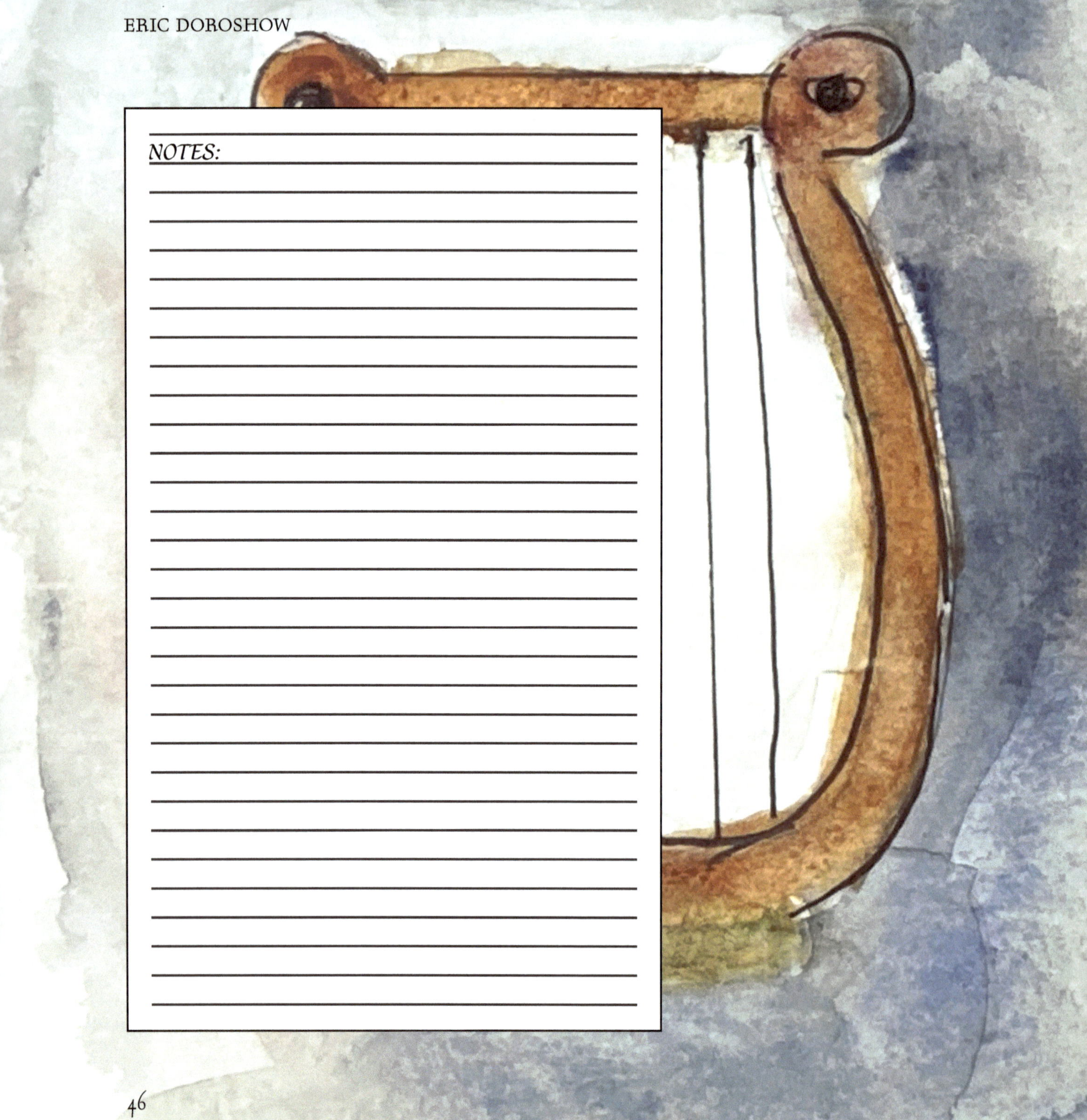

NOTES:

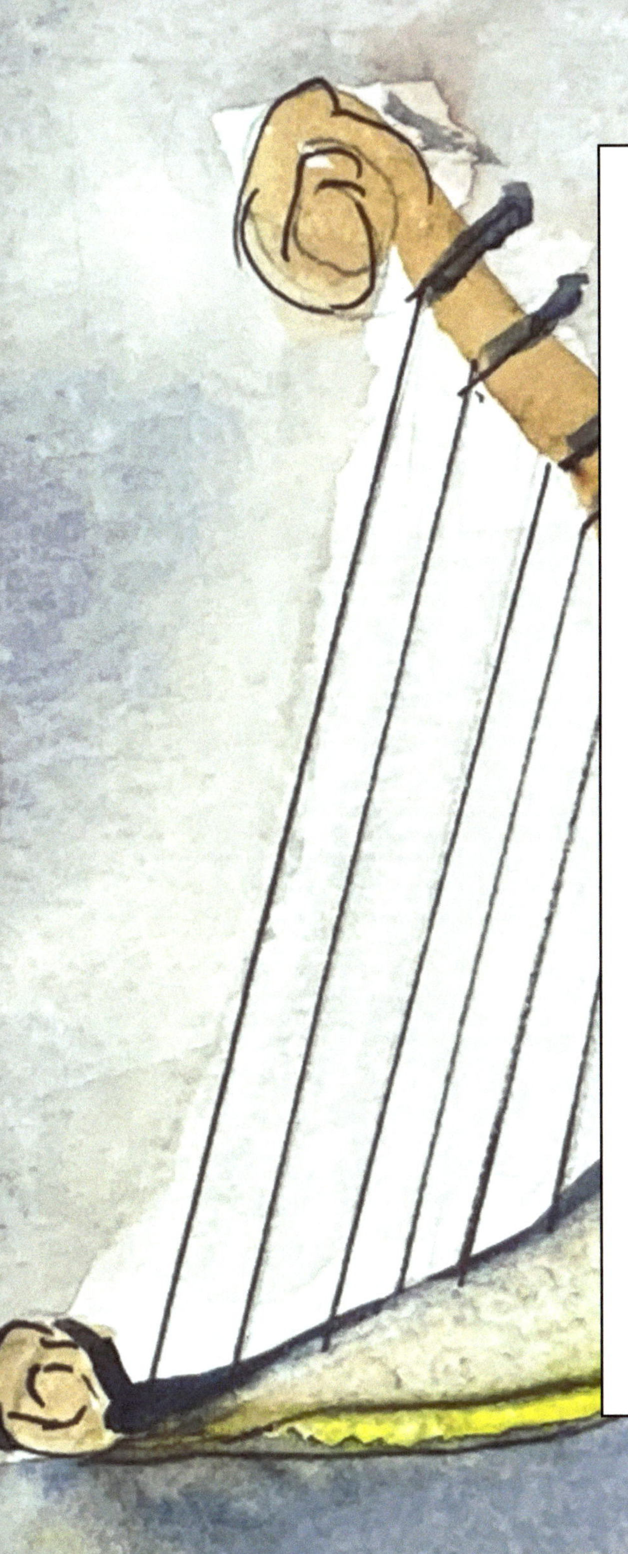

CHAPTER SEVEN

King David And Leadership

IN RECENT YEARS, King David's story has been used to show leaders and executives how to succeed in the business world. His ability to mobilize his supporters and lead was the subject of a book entitled *The Heart of an Executive: Lessons on Leadership from the Life of King David* by Richard D. Philips (Doubleday Publishing, 1999).

In this chapter, I've summarized some of the ideas of the author and applied them to my research on King David.

Today's leaders must instill confidence and assurance in the company's employees in times of trouble and threats. The story of David is full of instances where he helped others summon the courage to combat threat and turmoil. An instance of his leadership can be found in the

David and Goliath story where David was victorious against great odds.

Today's leaders must motivate by showing the company's employees that they belong to a cause greater than themselves. David demonstrated this trait. The Davidic Psalms show that there is a cause greater than the individual. The stories of David's battles show him as a motivator-in-chief. Again and again, he shows his unique ability to motivate troops and triumph over great odds. He built cohesion and a national sense of identity to The Twelve Tribes of Israel. Before David, each tribe was often indifferent to the other tribes. David brought the individual groups together and imbued them with the fortitude to work as a team to do great things as a united and powerful nation.

Some executives make bold statements about a future project for the organization, but when problems occur, they quickly backtrack. It becomes evident that they were never fully committed to the project. For example, we sometimes see new business projects being rolled along with broad pronouncements about how the project will foster the greater good of the organization. However, if the new project is not immediately successful, those same executives backtrack from the project, leaving employees confused.

David was genuinely and fully committed in his dealings. He did not back off at the first sign of trouble. He showed true commitment in what he did. Whether it was fighting battles or conquering Jerusalem and making it his capital of a united Israel, David was unwavering in his vision. His clear focus was inspirational to his soldiers and his subjects.

Even the most talented leaders will make mistakes, but some won't acknowledge these mistakes. They may seek to cover them up and not be truthful to those in the organization, or they blame others for their mistakes. Both King Saul and King David made mistakes during their respective reigns, but how they handled their mistakes is very telling.

In 1 Samuel 15:13, the Lord told the prophet Samuel to command Saul to destroy the Amalekites and all they owned. We discussed the Amalekites in Chapter 3. Saul did defeat them in battle, but did not follow the Lord's decree to utterly destroy all their possessions The choicest sheep and oxen were spared. When this error was brought to Saul's attention by Samuel, he argued that he committed no wrong. Instead of taking responsibility for his mistake, Saul blamed his own people for taking these things from the defeated foe. He compounded his error by lamely attempting to defend it, saying that these animals would be used for a great sacrifice to the Lord.

Conversely, David owned up to his mistakes and never tried to hide them. When it came time to acknowledge his mistakes, David did so with sincerity and commitment. He did not blame others for the errors he made, but instead took full responsibility for his actions. This trait can be seen throughout his life, including when he took full responsibility before the prophet Nathan for his misdeeds in the Bathsheba affair. "I have sinned against the Lord," said David in II Samuel 12:13.

Unfortunately, some executives put their own prestige and fortune above the organization. The

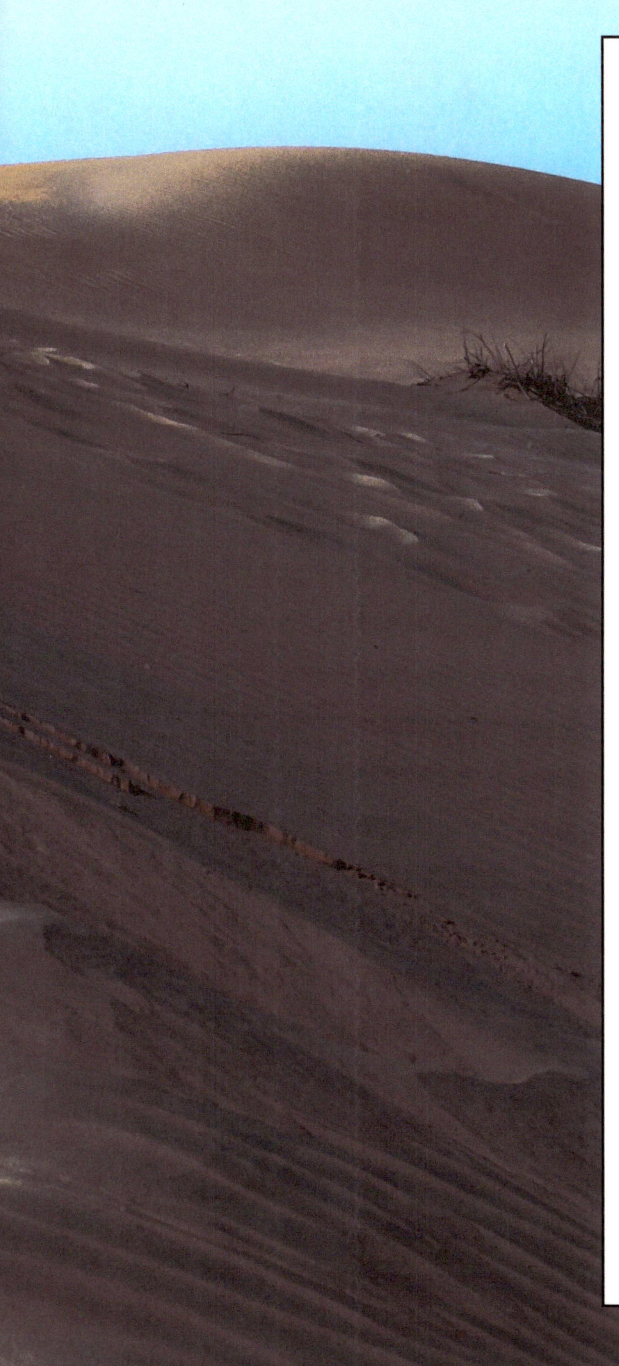

perceptions of others become more important than the good of the organization. As a result, some executives show envy and insecurity. Anger against subordinates sometimes follows. King Saul was such a man; through his reign, he showed these negative traits. However, throughout his reign, David tried to keep the best interests of the nation first and foremost. When he failed to do so, he sincerely made amends. This power of sincerity can be seen today in the Davidic Psalms.

Some leaders surround themselves with sycophants who give unending praise to the executive. David did not do that. He had the prophet Nathan to advise him. When Nathan told David he had sinned in the Bathsheba affair, he sincerely lived up to his mistakes. Rather than kill Nathan, he listened to him and asked G-d for sincere forgiveness.

Today's executives face unprecedented challenges in the workforce. New consumer tastes, the ever-changing impact of social media and supply chain challenges keep many executives up at night. The successful executive must find

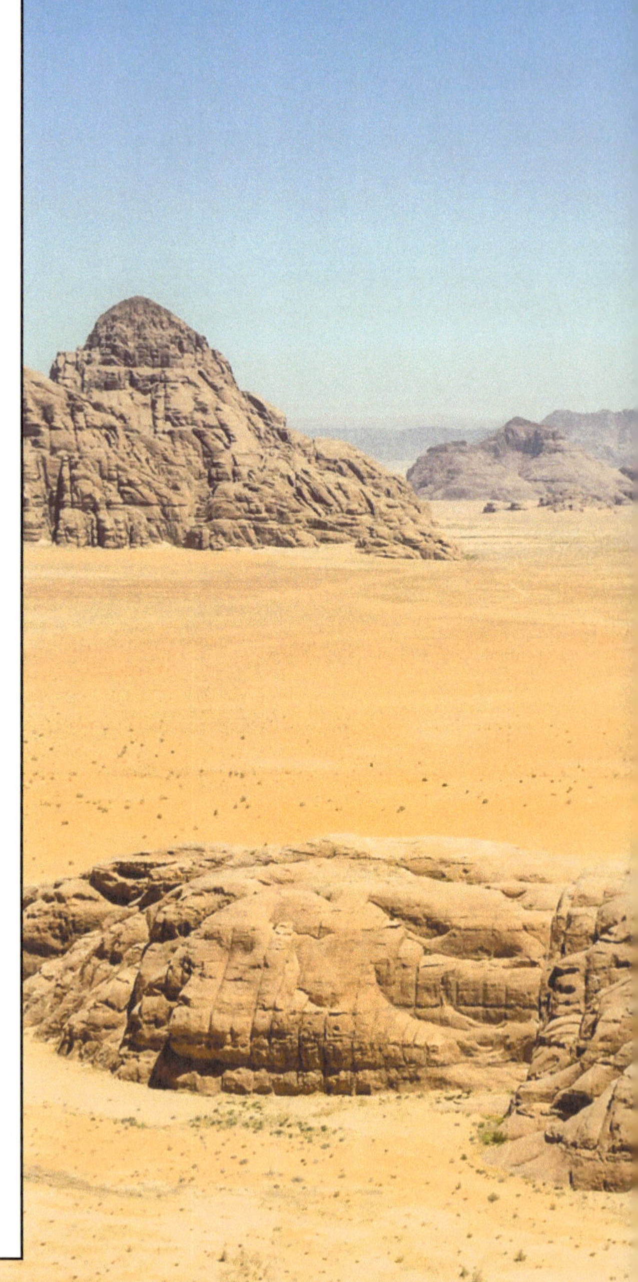

the innovations and tools in the organization and use them to achieve a strategic advantage. In the David and Goliath story, David showed innovation. He knew that Goliath was stronger and was well-schooled in the use of the sword. He could never have beaten Goliath in a sword fight. David had to find a better way to confront Goliath. He did this by perfecting an important innovation: using a slingshot in battle to kill a bigger and much stronger foe.

Strong executives need to be out front, leading others. Saul was not such a person and, as a result, the people lost faith in him. However, David was such a leader. He led his troops from the front during his campaigns.

To stay competitive, a leader must learn from their mistakes. Humility is critical in this process. David learned from his errors and humbly apologized for them. This can be seen quite clearly in the Davidic Psalms.

No matter how talented the executive is, things will go wrong. Sometimes all one can do is to hold on. David had many difficult periods in his life, but he held on and put his trust in

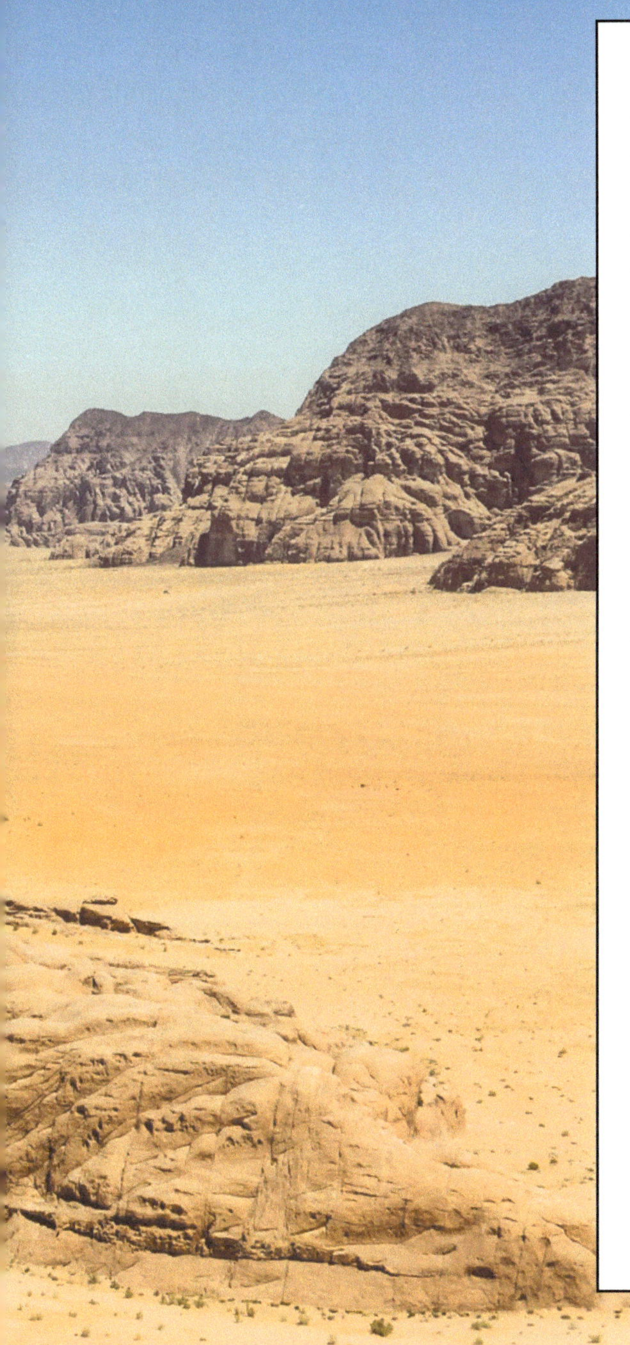

G-d. In bad times, it is natural to feel hatred and vengeance. Saul showed unmitigated hatred of David throughout his reign. David fought these negative emotions and showed himself to be a true, compassionate leader.

All executives must plan for succession. Without a clear plan, the company itself may fail. David planned for succession. He gave his son and successor, Solomon, clear advice about being strong. He lent his presence to the process, and authenticated Solomon's authority as he stepped forth to the throne. Solomon became a great king in part because of David's planning and help in the succession.

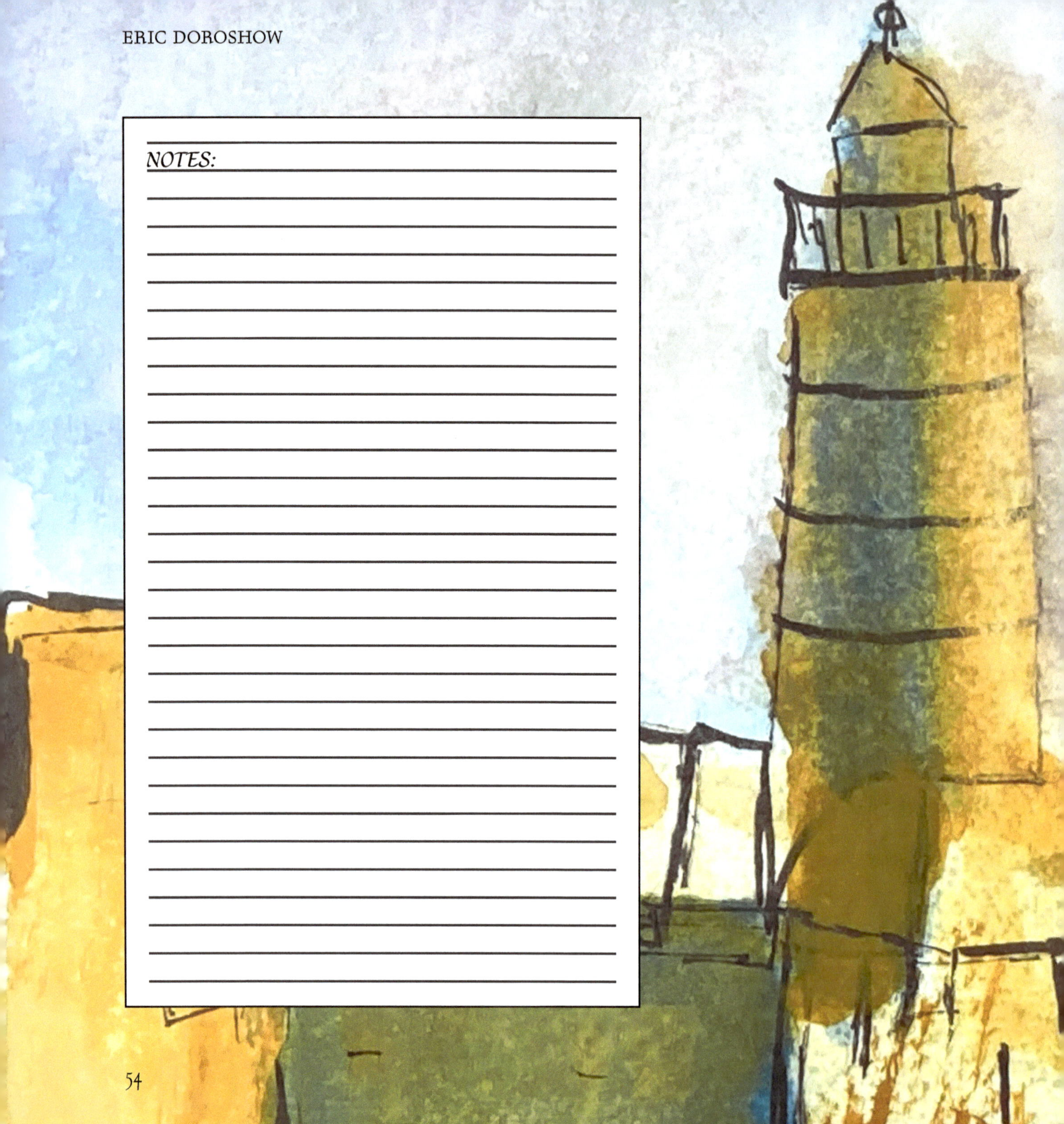

NOTES:

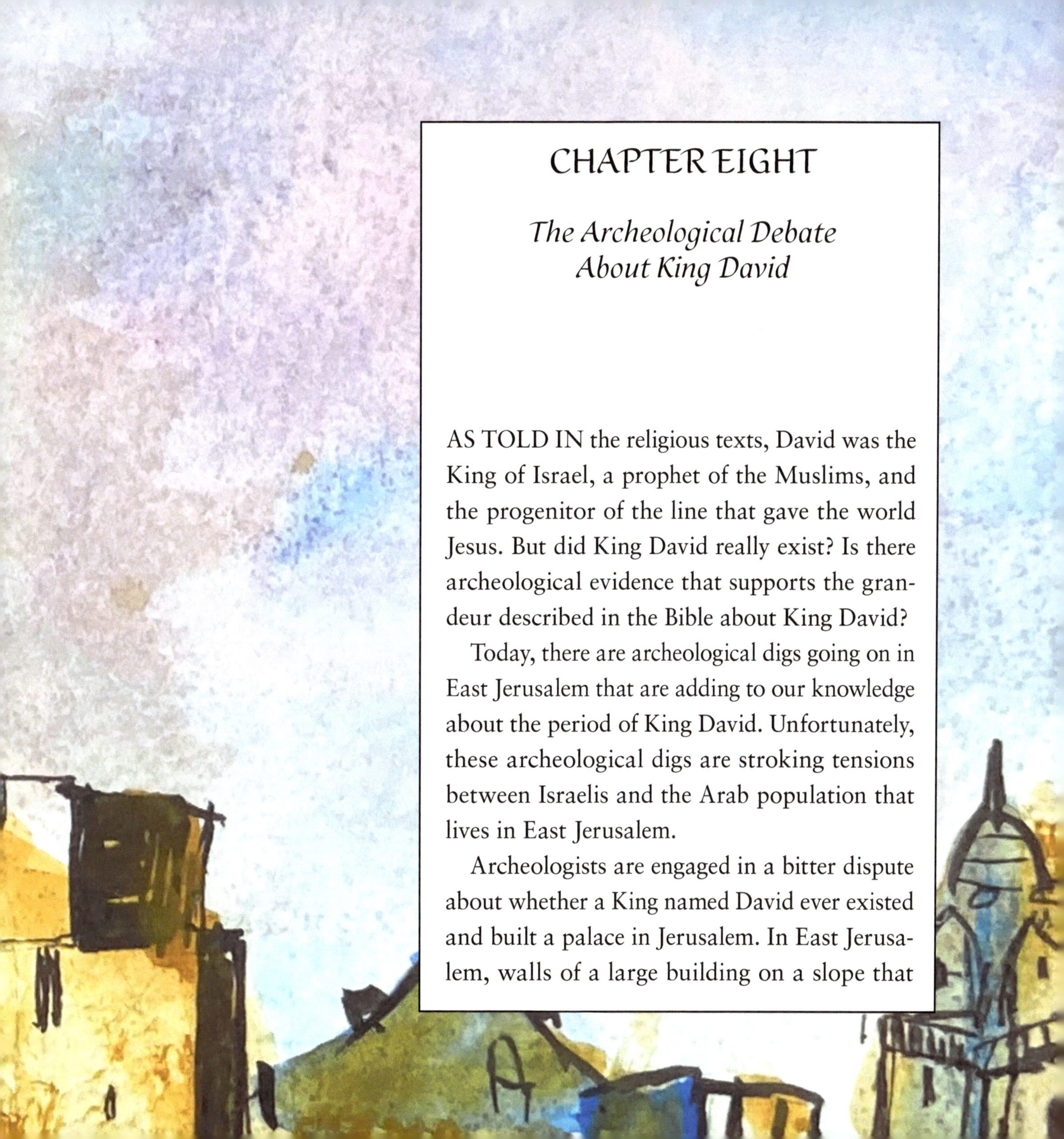

CHAPTER EIGHT

The Archeological Debate About King David

AS TOLD IN the religious texts, David was the King of Israel, a prophet of the Muslims, and the progenitor of the line that gave the world Jesus. But did King David really exist? Is there archeological evidence that supports the grandeur described in the Bible about King David?

Today, there are archeological digs going on in East Jerusalem that are adding to our knowledge about the period of King David. Unfortunately, these archeological digs are stroking tensions between Israelis and the Arab population that lives in East Jerusalem.

Archeologists are engaged in a bitter dispute about whether a King named David ever existed and built a palace in Jerusalem. In East Jerusalem, walls of a large building on a slope that descends from the Temple Mount were uncovered. This slope is known as the City of David. The slope is seen as consistent with the location discussed in the Book of Samuel, which describes the palace that the King of Tyre built for David. Many believe this is where King David resided. There have been other major finds in the area, including a royal seal called a bulla.

There are two schools of debate among archaeologists. One school, called the maximalists, was led by Yigael Yadin, who was one of Israel's leading archeologists in the 1950s. His current followers are Yosef Garfinkel and Eilat Mazar. They believe that the findings from the archeological digs, like the one where the bulla was found, proved the validity of many stories in the Bible. They treat the Bible as verifiable fact. They believe that the ruins they have found in the City of David prove that King David really existed.

The other school, called the minimalists, is skeptical about the value of the current archeological finds in the City of David. This group is led by Israel Finkelstein. He accuses the maximalists of being led astray by "irrelevant sentiments." In his writings, Finkelstein contested the significance of the ruins in the City of David. His thinking is that King David, if he existed at all, had only minor significance. At best, he served as a vassal to the Omride Kingdom, and the biblical story of David contains only kernels of truth, being preserved as a tale that was handed down through the generations.

Both sides almost all agree on one thing: that the 11-acre mound in Jerusalem was the seat of David's dynasty, and was the beginning of what we now call Jewish Civilization. "In search of King David's Lost Empire" by Ruth Margalit, *The New Yorker Magazine*, June 22, 2020 edition.

According to an article published in *Haaretz* on November 21, 2017 entitled "Did David and Solomon's United Monarchy Exist? Vast Ancient Mining Operations May Hold Answers", some archeologists point to the mines in the Aravah desert in southern Israel as proof that David existed. During the 10th century B.C.E., there was massive copper production at Timna, located

300 kilometers south of Jerusalem in the desert. The mines are in the very territory the Bible says David won from the Edomites, who became subject to Israel II Samuel 8:13-14. If King David was a historical figure, he would have needed copper for agricultural tools and weapons. Because the mines were huge, they would have required the support of a major political figure like King David to make them successful.

Archeologists recently unveiled a large archeological find 32 kilometers south of Jerusalem at a site called Khirbet Qeiyafa. The maximalists believe that this is where a mighty Judaic city was located dating to the time of David. They believe the size of this city proves that David existed and had a large kingdom, but the minimalists disagree.

In 1993, the minimalists suffered a setback. Israeli archeologists working near the Syrian border found a fragment of a rock dating from the 9th century B.C.E. It was part of a structure likely erected by the King of Aram, named Hazael. The inscription on the rock describes the defeat of the kingdoms of Judah and Israel by

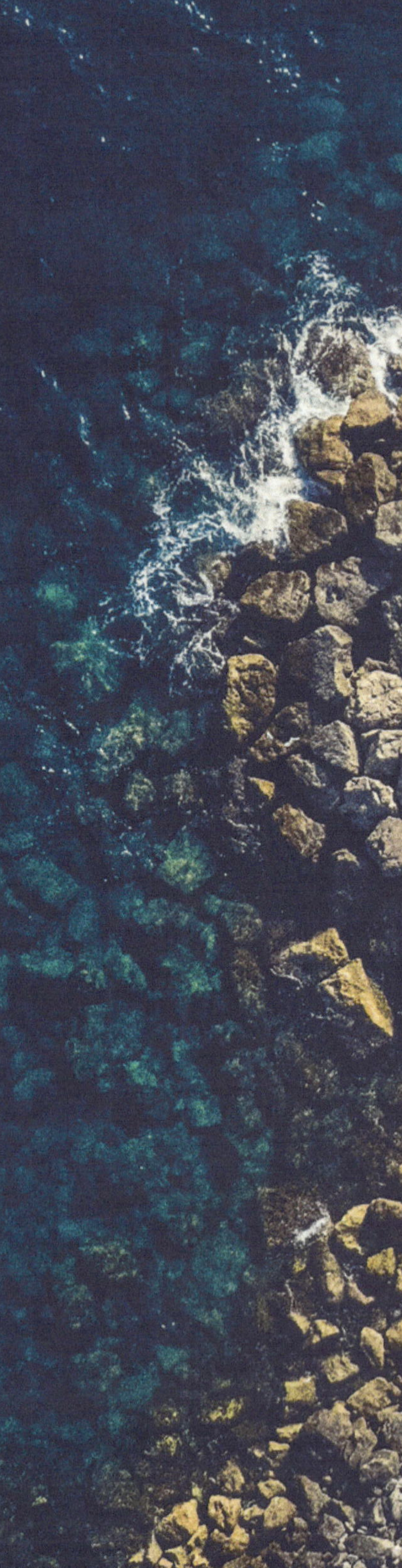

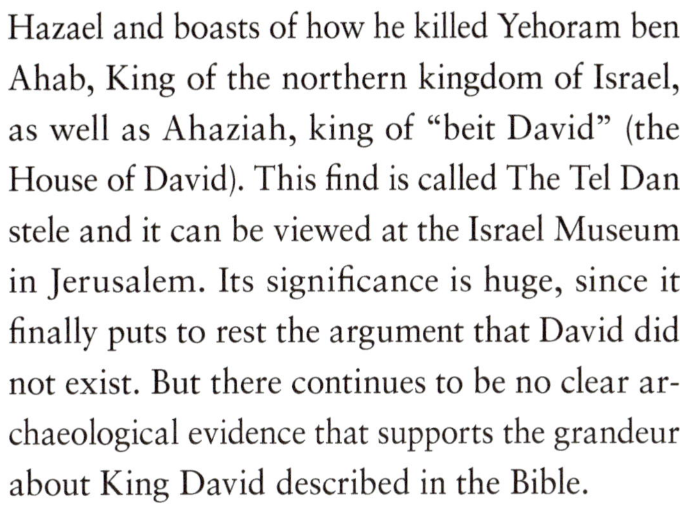

Hazael and boasts of how he killed Yehoram ben Ahab, King of the northern kingdom of Israel, as well as Ahaziah, king of "beit David" (the House of David). This find is called The Tel Dan stele and it can be viewed at the Israel Museum in Jerusalem. Its significance is huge, since it finally puts to rest the argument that David did not exist. But there continues to be no clear archaeological evidence that supports the grandeur about King David described in the Bible.

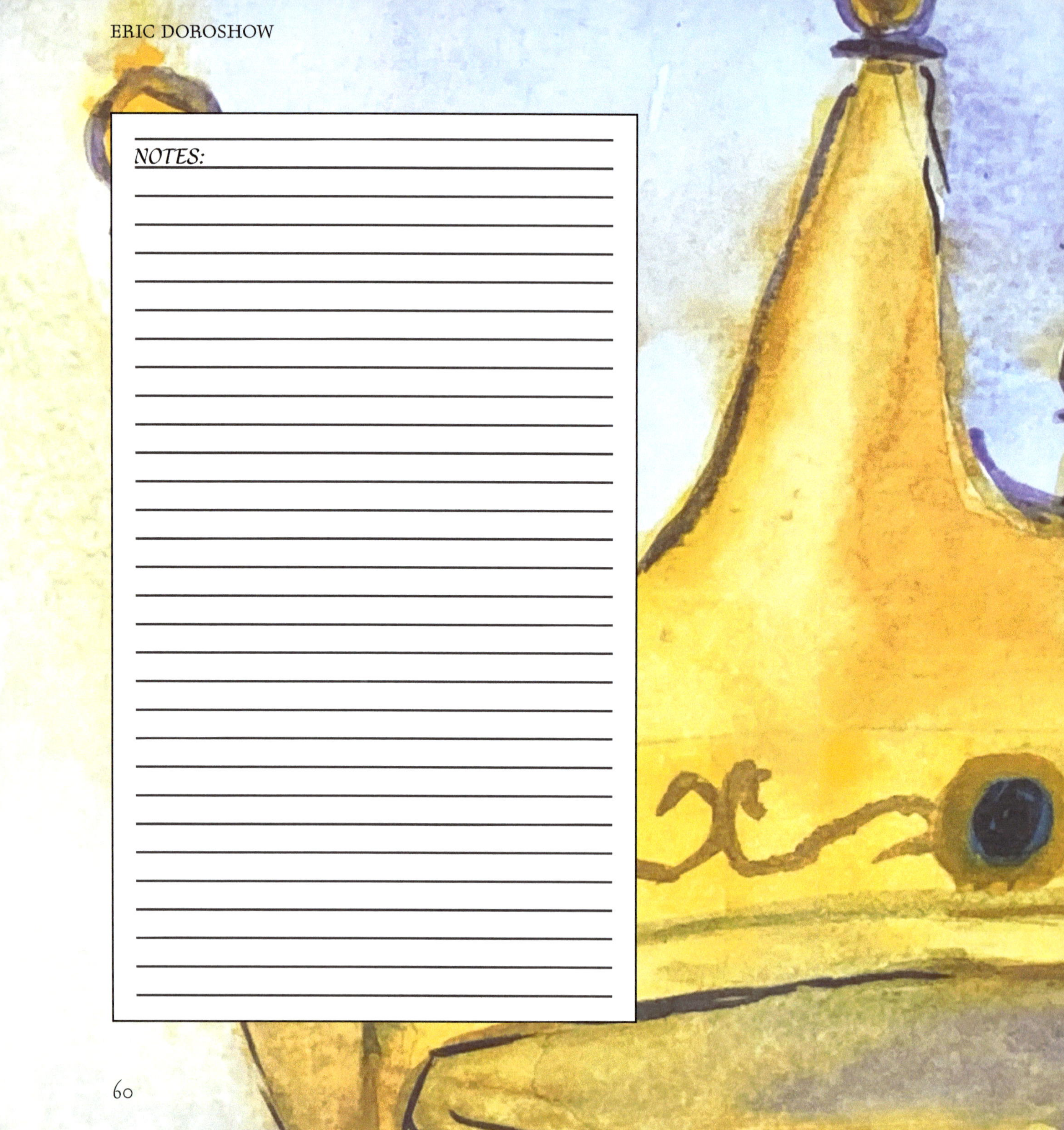

NOTES:

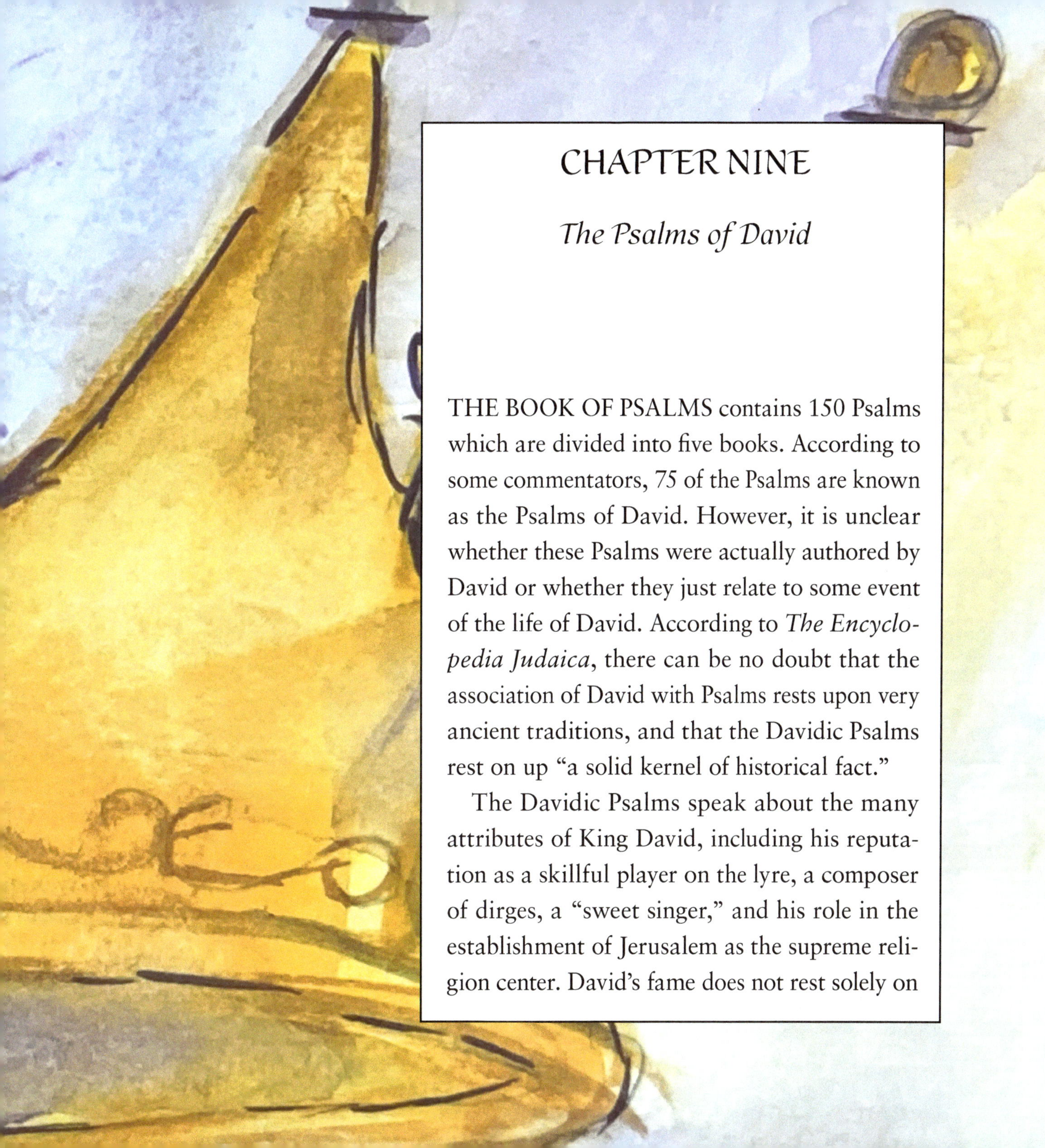

CHAPTER NINE

The Psalms of David

THE BOOK OF PSALMS contains 150 Psalms which are divided into five books. According to some commentators, 75 of the Psalms are known as the Psalms of David. However, it is unclear whether these Psalms were actually authored by David or whether they just relate to some event of the life of David. According to *The Encyclopedia Judaica*, there can be no doubt that the association of David with Psalms rests upon very ancient traditions, and that the Davidic Psalms rest on up "a solid kernel of historical fact."

The Davidic Psalms speak about the many attributes of King David, including his reputation as a skillful player on the lyre, a composer of dirges, a "sweet singer," and his role in the establishment of Jerusalem as the supreme religion center. David's fame does not rest solely on

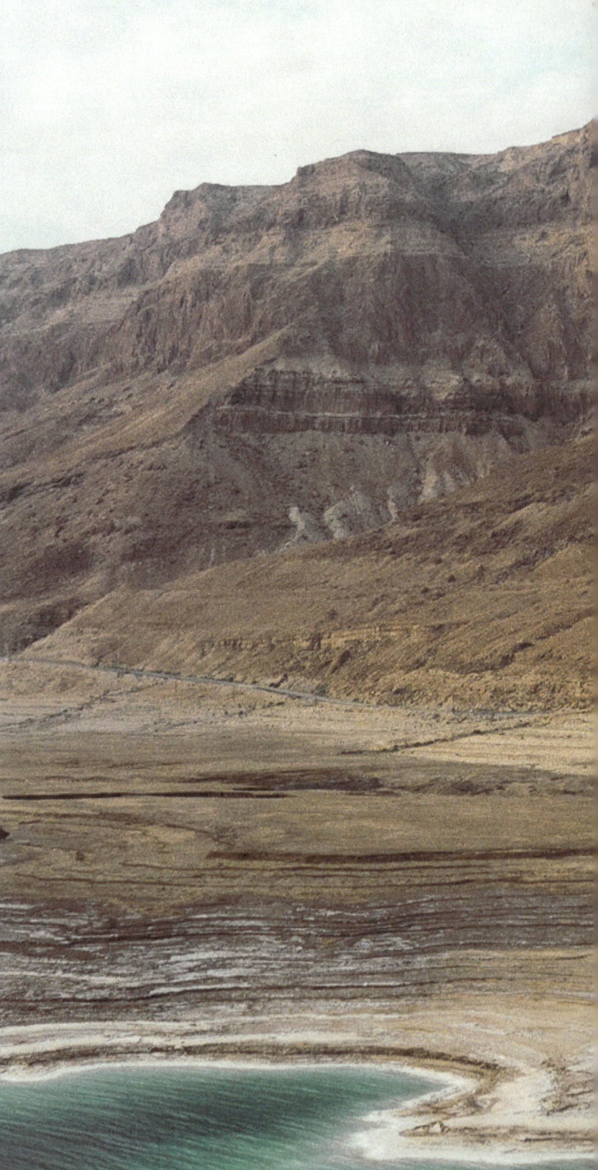

the fact that he was a great warrior and ruler. It also rests on his poetry contained in the Book of Palms.

According to *Chabad.org*:

"The Psalms are hymns of praise to the Almighty G-d, Creator of the Universe. They speak of G-d's greatness, His goodness and mercy; His power and justice. David pours out his heart in these Psalms and avows his sincerest and purest trust in G-d alone. Many of the Psalms are prayers and supplications to G-d which King David prayed in times of trouble. Some Psalms contain good advice, showing the way of true happiness through virtue and the fulfillment of G-d's commandments.

Thus, the Psalms reflect all the varied incidents that can happen in life, both to the individual and to the whole Jewish nation. Indeed, in the history of David—his exile, persecution, struggles, and eventual triumph—the Jewish people, collectively and individually, find an example and prophecy of their own life. No wonder the Book of Psalms has throughout the ages served as a boundless source of inspiration, courage, and hope."

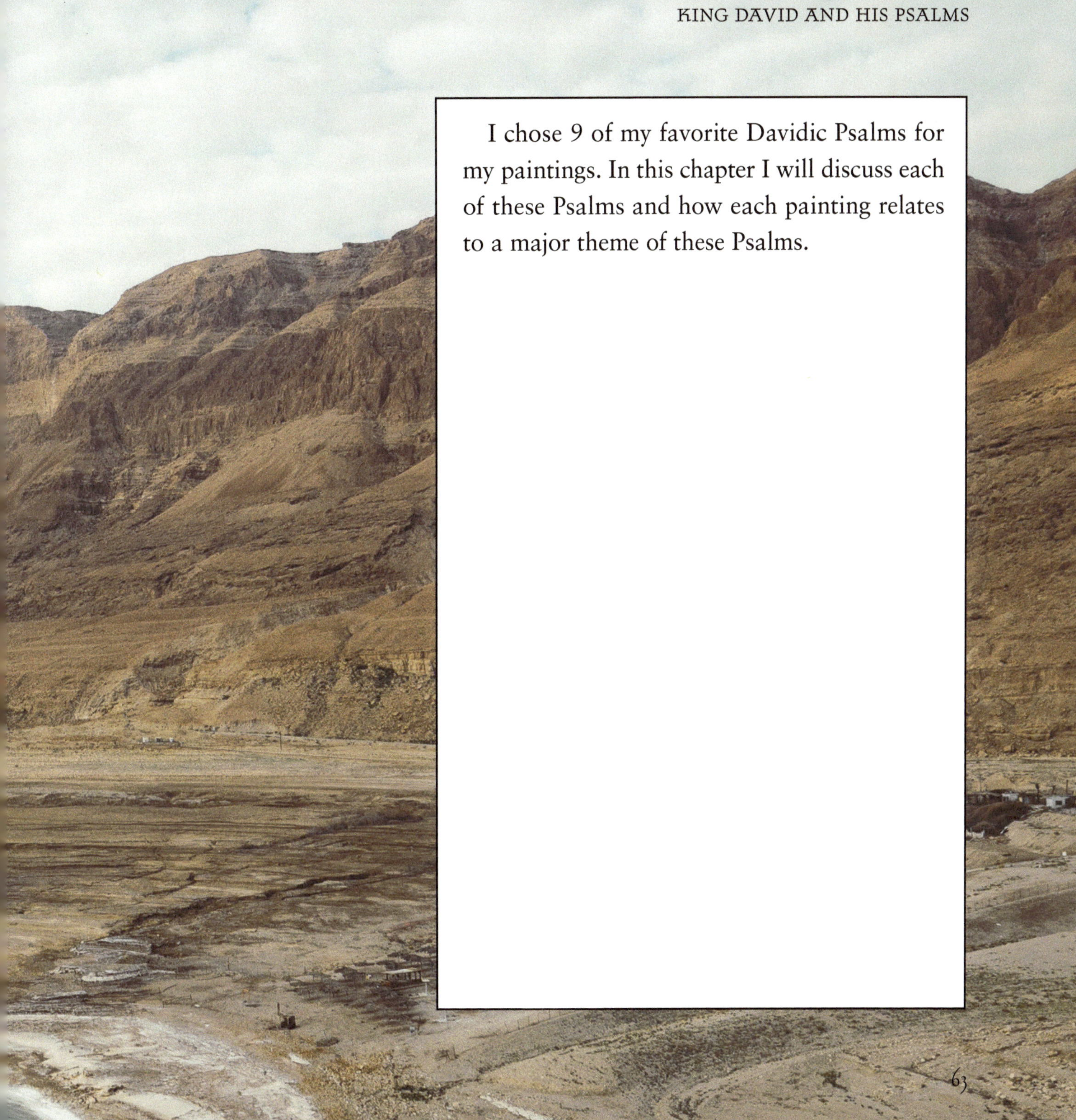

I chose 9 of my favorite Davidic Psalms for my paintings. In this chapter I will discuss each of these Psalms and how each painting relates to a major theme of these Psalms.

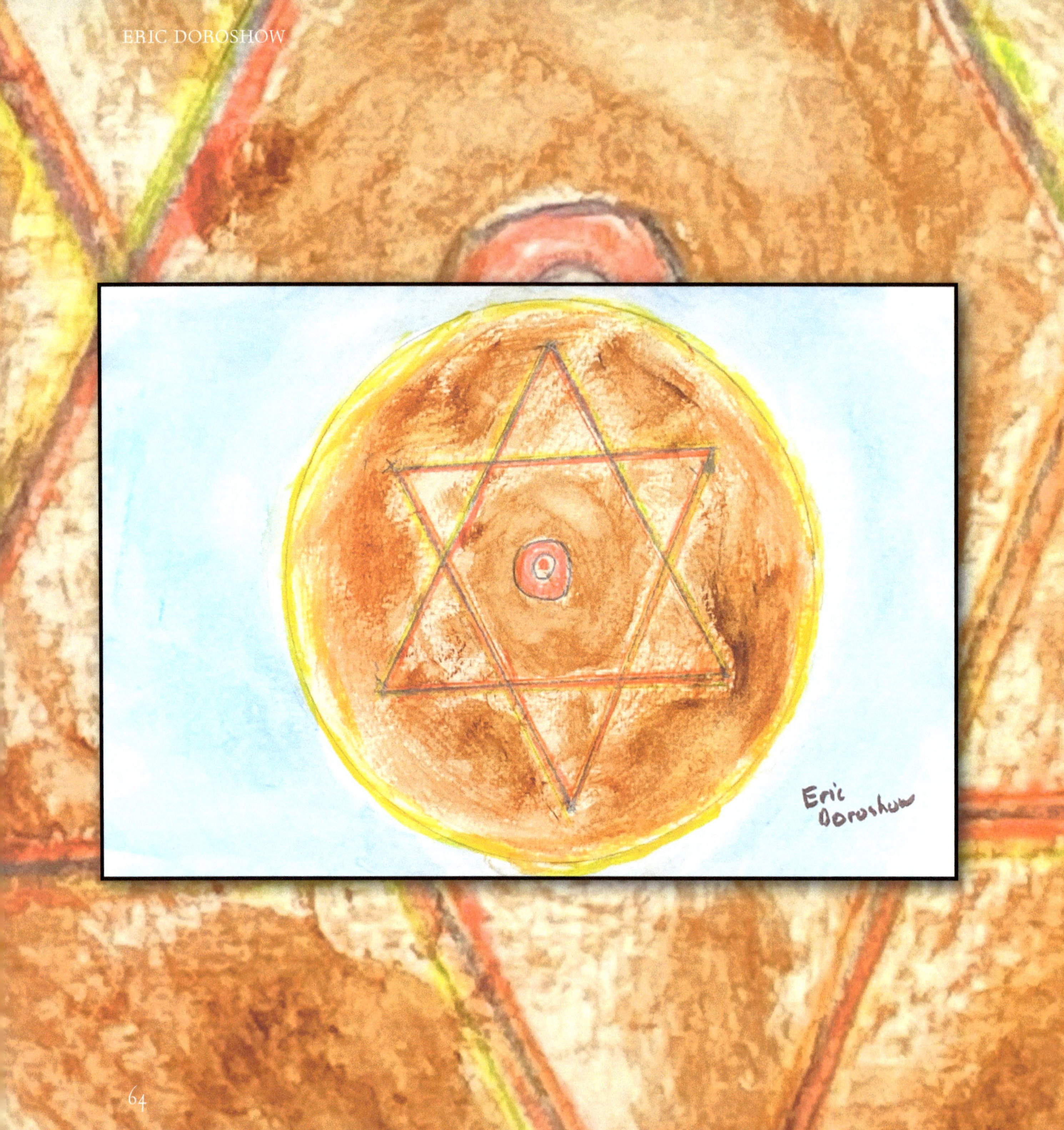
Eric
Doroshow

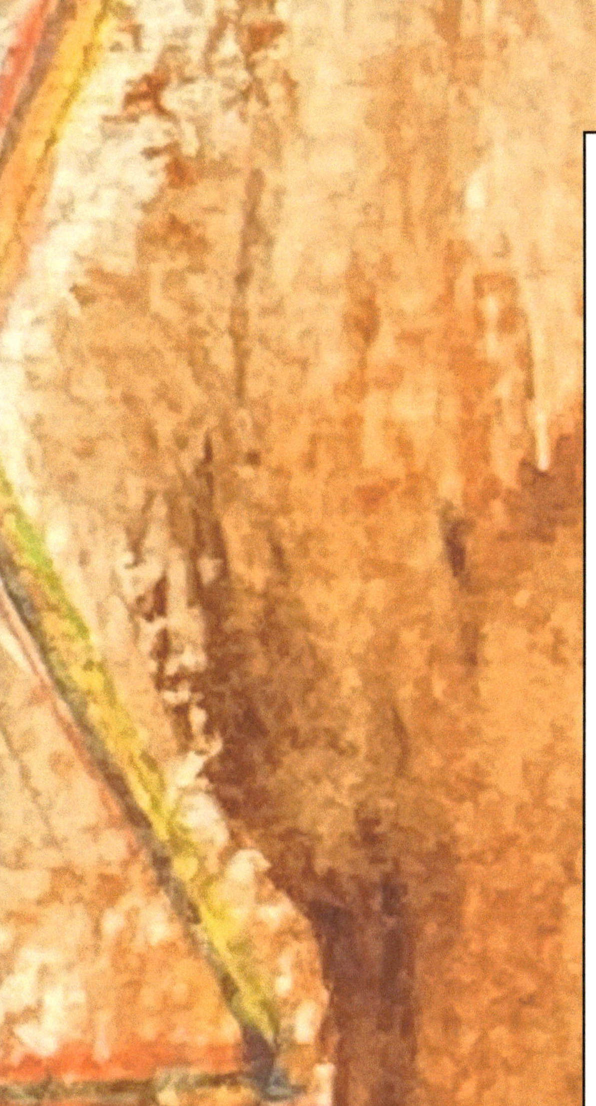

Psalm 3

1 A song of David, when he fled from
Absalom his son.
2 O Lord, how many have my adversaries become! Great men rise up
against me.
3 Great men say concerning my soul,
"He has no salvation in G-d to
eternity."
4 But You, O Lord, are a shield about
me, my glory and He Who raises up
my head.
5 With my voice, I call to the Lord,
and He answered me from His holy
mount to eternity.
6 I lay down and slept; I awoke, for
the Lord will support me.
7 I will not fear ten thousands of people, who have set themselves against
me all around.
8 Arise, O Lord, save me, my G-d, for
You have struck all my enemies on
the cheek; You have broken the teeth
of the wicked.
9 It is incumbent upon the Lord to
save, and it is incumbent upon Your
people to bless You forever.

According to the *Jewish Virtual Library*:

"Prior to going to sleep, many Jews recite some, if not all, of the following prayers which are believed to bring peace and comfort to one as they sleep. Scholars used to teach that during the night demons come searching for innocent souls; however, completing these prayers would protect the[m] from such dangers. The bedtime prayers are structured around the *Shema*, which many Jews believe will protect them for the afterlife if they unexpectedly die while sleeping." Psalm 3 is one of those prayers.

My painting picks up the theme in Verse 4 that the Lord is a "shield about me." The shield picked for the painting is the Star of David. This hexagram is a commonly used symbol of Judaism today.

The history of the Star of David is unclear. There is a legend that the Star decorated the shields of King David's army. According to The Jewish Virtual Library, in the Middle Ages the shield was used in both Christian and Muslim countries. Arab sources called it "the seal of Solomon." It first began appearing in some

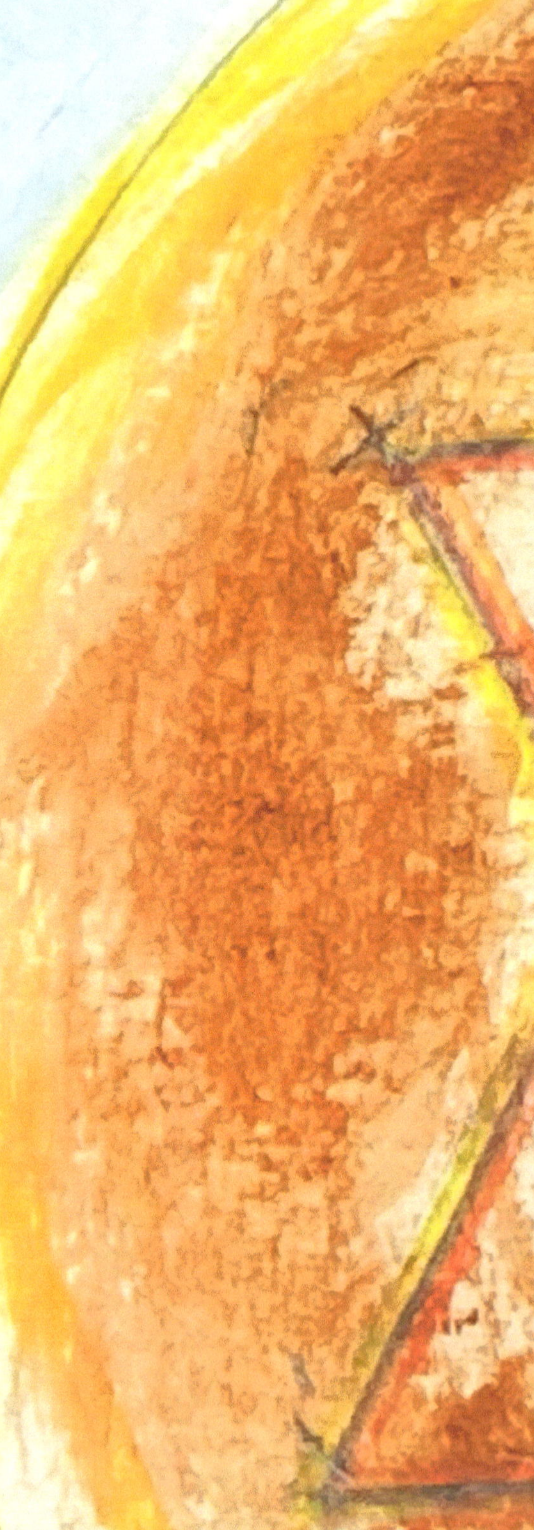

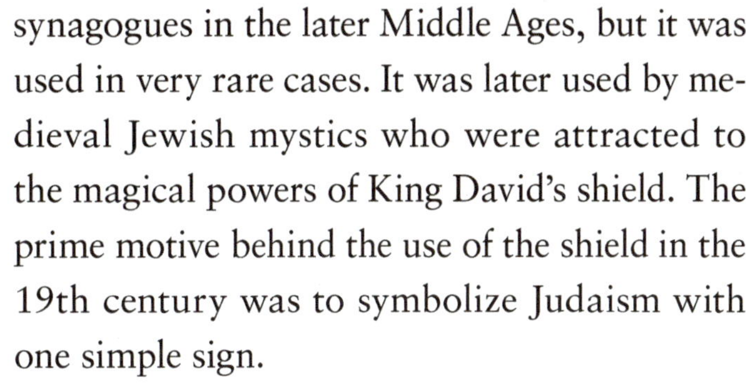

synagogues in the later Middle Ages, but it was used in very rare cases. It was later used by medieval Jewish mystics who were attracted to the magical powers of King David's shield. The prime motive behind the use of the shield in the 19th century was to symbolize Judaism with one simple sign.

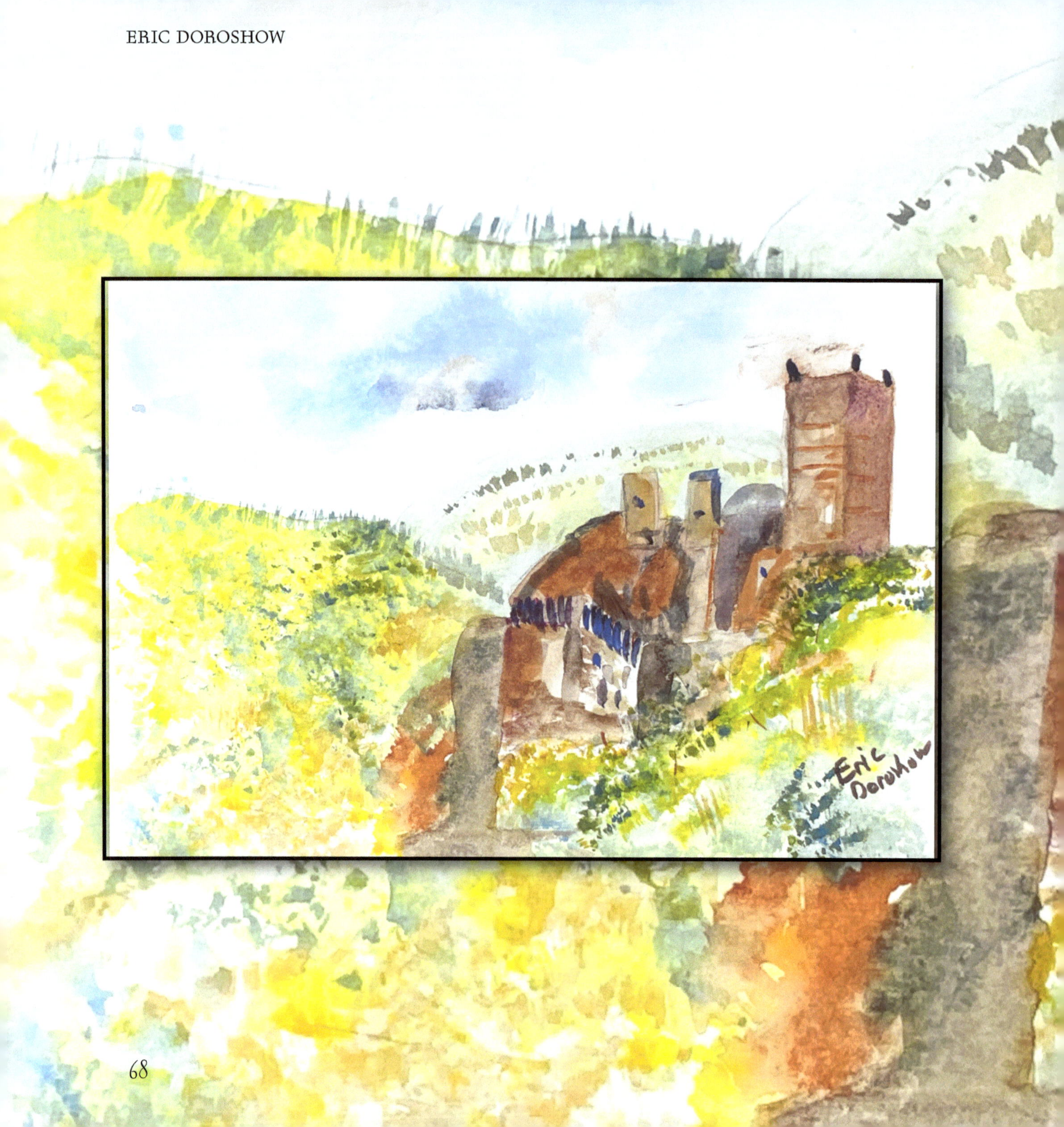
Eric
Doroshow

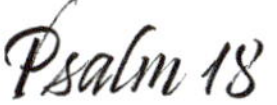

1 For the conductor; of the servant of the Lord, of David, who spoke to the Lord the words of this song on the day that the Lord saved him from the hand of all his enemies and from the hand of Saul.

2 And he said, "I love You, O Lord, my strength.

3 O Lord, my rock and my fortress and my rescuer; my G-d, my rock, I will take refuge in Him; my shield and the horn of my salvation, my refuge.

4 With praise I call to the Lord, and from my enemies I will be saved.

5 Bands of death have encompassed me, and streams of scoundrels would affright me.

6 Bands of the nether world have surrounded me; the snares of death confronted me.

7 When I am in distress, I call upon the Lord; yes, I cry out to my G-d; out of His temple He hears my voice, and my cry comes before Him in His ears.

8 The earth shook and quaked, the
foundations of the mountains did
tremble; and they were shaken when
He was angered.
9 Smoke went up in His nostrils, and
fire out of His mouth did devour;
coals flamed forth from Him.
10 And He bent the heavens, and He
came down, and thick darkness was
under His feet.
11 And He rode on a cherub and did
fly; He swooped on the wings of the
wind.
12 He made darkness His hiding-place
about Him as His booth; the darkness
of waters, thick clouds of the skies.
13 From the brightness before Him,
His thick cloud passed, hail and coals
of fire.
14 The Lord thundered from Heaven;
and the Most High gave forth His
voice with hail and coals of fire.
15 And He sent out arrows and He
scattered them; He shot lightning and
He discomfited them.
16 And the depths of the water ap-
peared; the foundations of the world
were laid bare by Your rebuke, O

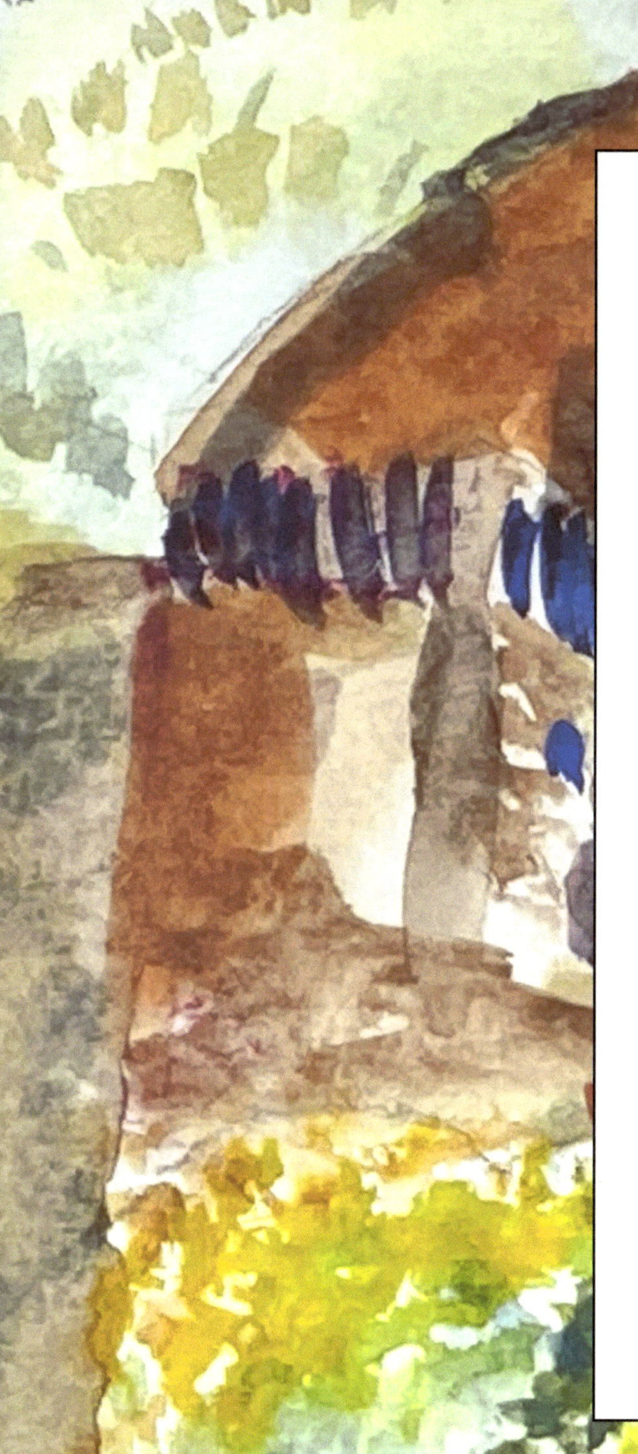

Lord, by the blast of the breath of
Your nostrils.
17 He sent forth from on high [and]
He took me; He drew me out of many
waters.
18 He delivered me from my mighty
enemy, and from those that hated me,
for they were too powerful for me.
19 They confronted me on the day of
my calamity, but the Lord was a support to me.
20 And He brought me forth into a
wide space; He delivered me because
He took delight in me.
21 The Lord rewarded me according
to my righteousness; according to
the cleanness of my hands He recompensed me.
22 For I have kept the ways of the Lord
and have not wickedly departed from
[the commandments of] my G-d.
23 For all His ordinances were before
me; and His statutes I will not remove
from myself.
24 And I was single-hearted with Him,
and I kept myself from my iniquity.
25 And the Lord has recompensed
me according to my righteousness,

according to the cleanness of my
hands before His eyes.
26 With a kind one, You show Yourself
kind, with a sincere man, You show
Yourself sincere.
27 With a pure one, You show Yourself
pure, but with a crooked one, You
deal crookedly.
28 For You deliver a humble people,
and You humble haughty eyes.
29 For You light my lamp; the Lord,
my G-d, does light my darkness.
30 For by You I run upon a troop, and
by my G-d I scale a wall.
31 [He is] the G-d Whose way is perfect; the word of the Lord is refined;
He is a shield to all who trust in Him.
32 For who is G-d save the Lord? And
who is a Rock, save our G-d?
33 The G-d is He Who girds me with
strength; and He makes my way
perfect.
34 He makes my feet like hinds, and
sets me upon my high places.
35 He trains my hands for war so that
a copper bow is bent by my arms.
36 You have given me the shield of
Your salvation; Your right hand has

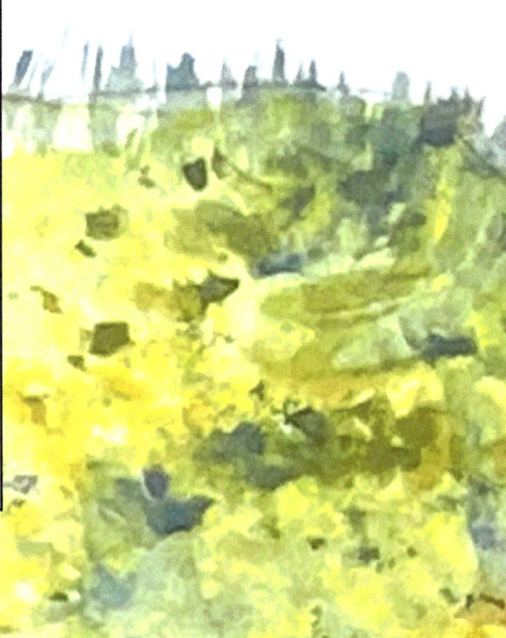

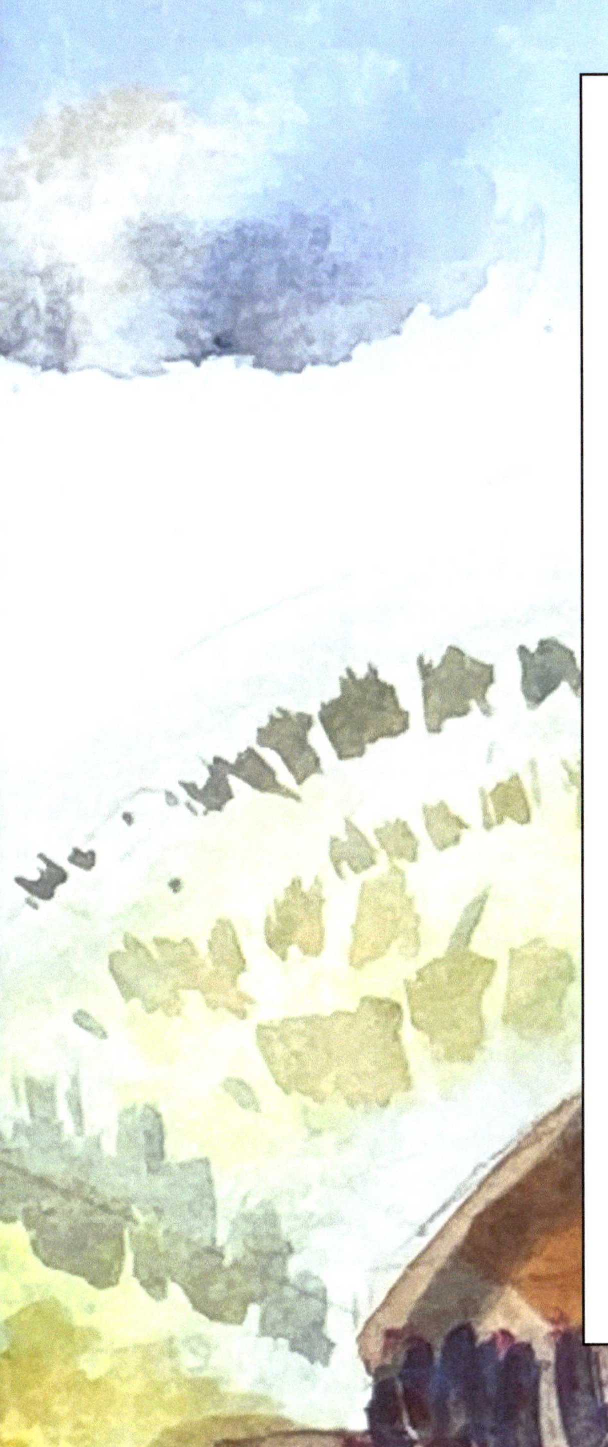

supported me, and You have treated
me with great humility.
37 You have enlarged my step[s] be-
neath me, and my ankles have not
slipped.
38 I have pursued my enemies and
overtaken them, never turning back
until they were consumed.
39 I have crushed them so that they
cannot rise; yea, they are fallen under
my feet.
40 For You have girded me with
strength for the battle; You have
subdued under me those that rose up
against me.
41 And of my enemies, You have given
me the back of their necks; those that
hate me, that I may cut them off.
42 They pray but no one saves them;
[even] to the Lord, but He answered
them not.
43 Then I ground them as dust before
the wind; as the mud in the streets I
did pour them.
44 You allowed me to escape from the
contenders of the people; You shall
make me the head over nations; may
a people that I do not know serve me.

45 As soon as they hear they shall obey
me; foreigners shall lie to me.
46 Foreigners shall wither, and they
shall fear their imprisonments.
47 The Lord lives, and blessed be my
Rock, and exalted be the G-d of my
salvation.
48 The G-d Who grants me vengeance
and destroys peoples instead of me.
49 Who delivers me from my enemies;
even above those that rise against me
You have lifted me; from the violent
man You deliver me.
50 Therefore, I will give thanks to You,
O Lord, among the nations, and to
Your name I will sing praises.
51 He gives great salvations to His
king, and He performs kindness to
His anointed; to David and to his
seed forever.

Psalm 18 is the longest Psalm according to *The New Psalm, The Psalms as Literature* by Benjamin J. Segal. It is one of the foremost Palms of the warrior-king. There is a strong usage of metaphors in the Psalm. Fire, smoke, thick clouds, and blazing coals create a fearsome picture of

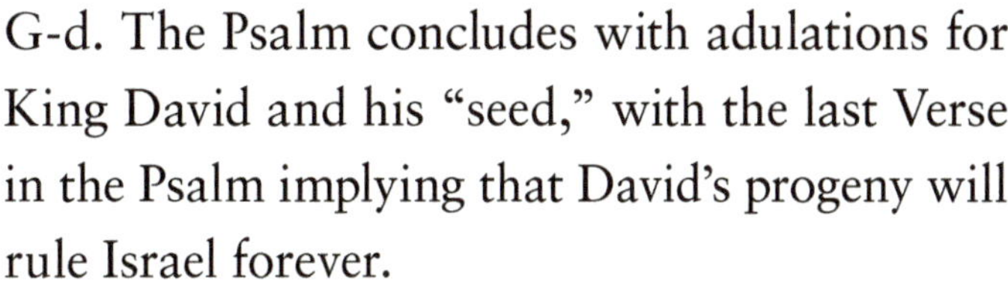

G-d. The Psalm concludes with adulations for King David and his "seed," with the last Verse in the Psalm implying that David's progeny will rule Israel forever.

My watercolor picks up the metaphor in Verse 3 that "the Lord is my fortress." My painting portrays a fortress on a hill.

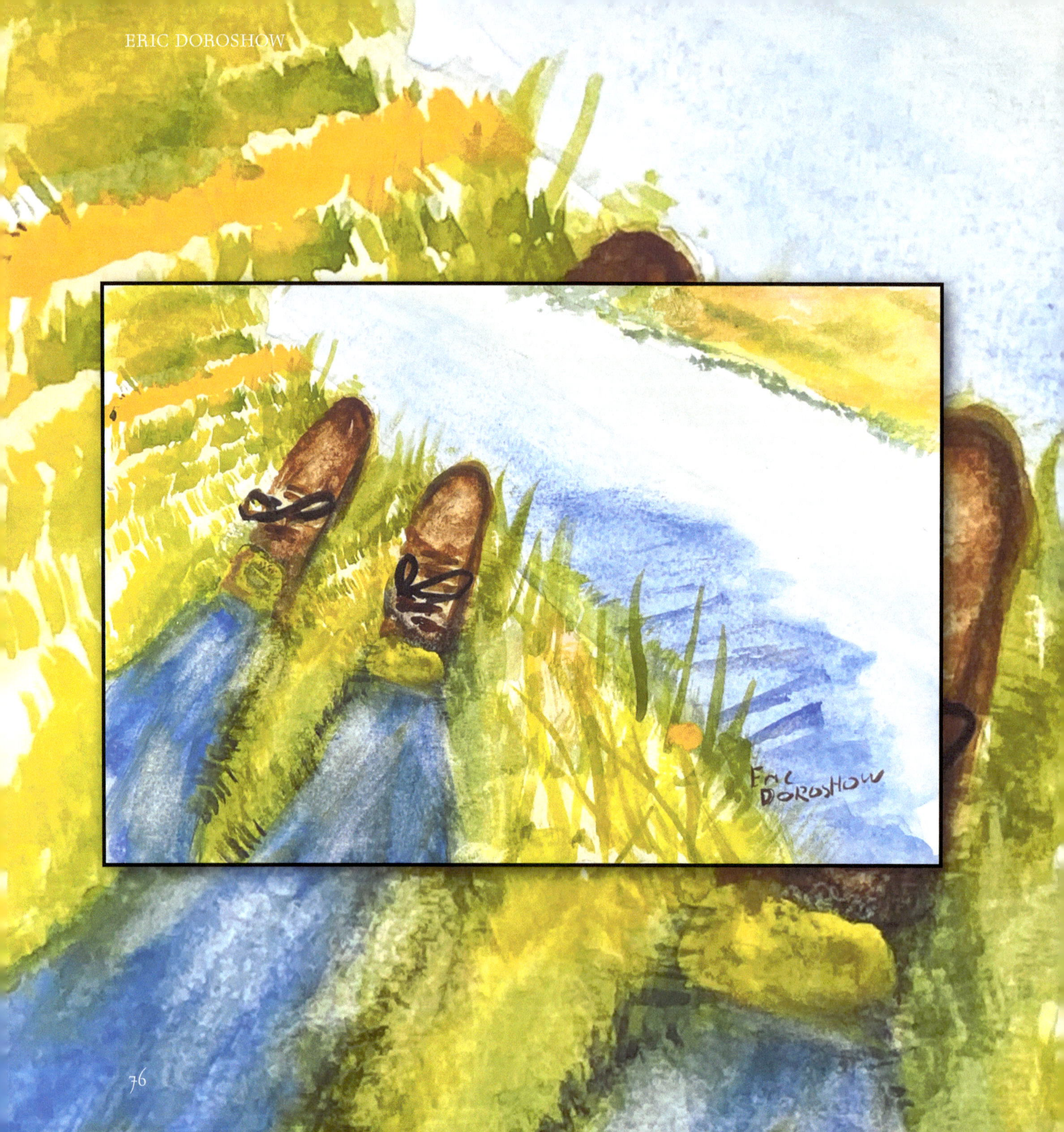
Eric
Doroshow

Psalm 23

[1] A song of David. The Lord is my
shepherd; I shall not want.
[2] He causes me to lie down in green
pastures; He leads me beside still
waters.
[3] He restores my soul; He leads me in
paths of righteousness for His name's
sake.
[4] Even when I walk in the valley of the
valley of darkness, I will fear no evil
for You are with me; Your rod and
Your staff - they comfort me.
[5] You set a table before me in the presence of my adversaries; You anointed
my head with oil; my cup overflows.
[6] May only goodness and kindness
pursue me all the days of my life, and
I will dwell in the house of the Lord
for length of days.

Psalm 23 is one of the best-known Psalms. In beautiful, poetic language it shows the commitment of David to The Lord. Various symbols are used in the Psalm. G-d is seen as a shepherd; David is seen as the sheep.

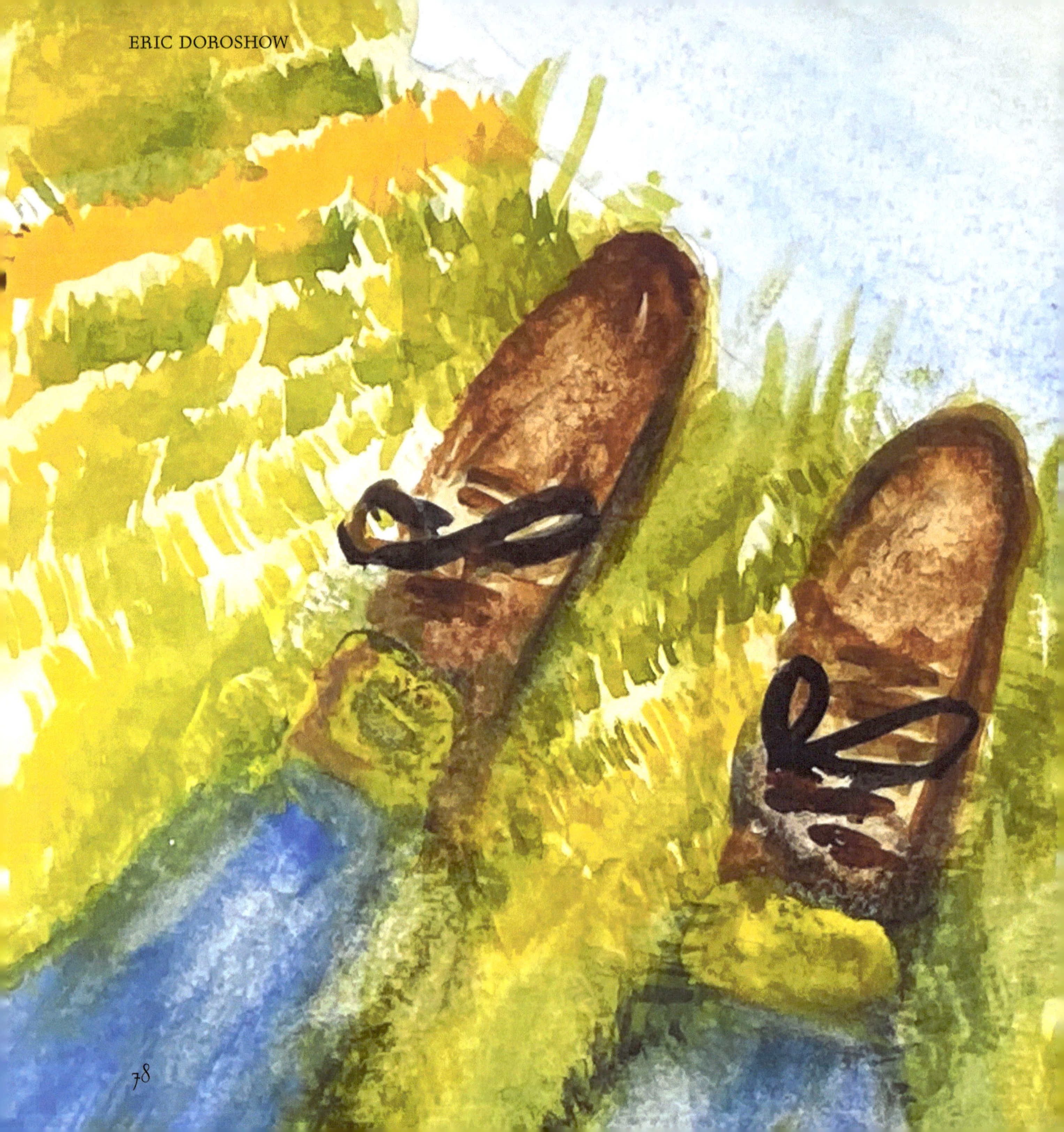

A famous French medieval rabbi, named Rashi, writes that David composed this Psalm while on the run from King Saul, who was intent on murdering him while he hid in the desert. He was on the brink of death without food or drink and then was miraculously saved by the Lord. As a result, David gratefully burst out in song, describing the magnitude of his trust in the Lord.

The Psalm has a fundamental role in Jewish liturgy. It is often recited in times of trouble, it is part of a set of Psalms recited on behalf of a sick person, and it is recited many times during the Jewish Sabbath.

In my painting, I referred to Verse 2. I painted the legs of a man who's reclining on a green pasture next to a stream. He is lying down by the still waters.

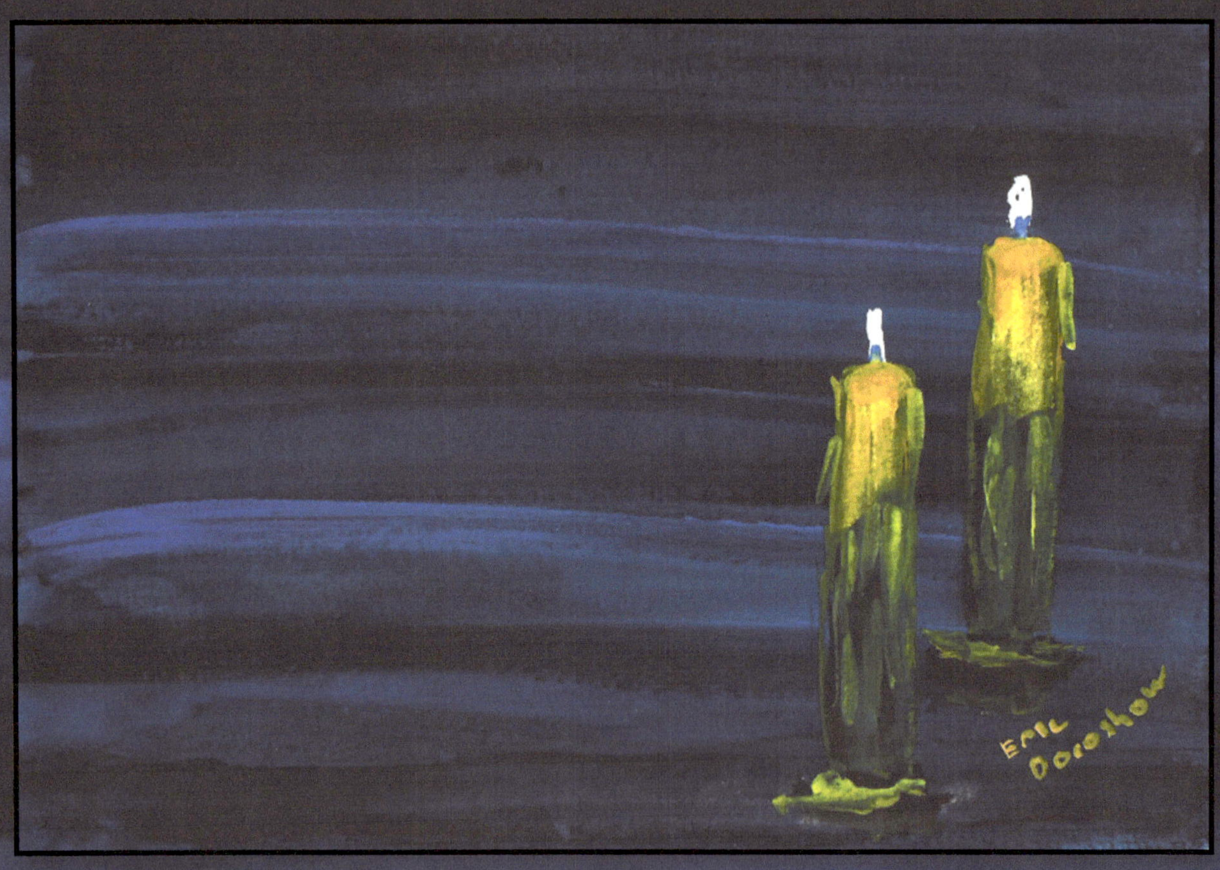
Eric
Doroshow

Psalm 27

1 Of David. The Lord is my light and
my salvation; whom shall I fear? The
Lord is the stronghold of my life;
from whom shall I be frightened?
2 When evildoers draw near to me to
devour my flesh, my adversaries and
my enemies against me-they stumbled
and fell.
3 If a camp encamps against me, my
heart shall not fear; if a war should
rise up against me, in this I trust.
4 One [thing] I ask of the Lord, that
I seek-that I may dwell in the house
of the Lord all the days of my life, to
see the pleasantness of the Lord and
to visit His Temple every morning.
5 That He will hide me in His taber-
nacle on the day of calamity; He will
conceal me in the secrecy of His tent;
He will lift me up on a rock.
6 And now, my head will be raised
over my enemies around me, and I
will sacrifice in His tent sacrifices
with joyous song; I will sing and
chant praise to the Lord.
7 Hearken, O Lord, to my voice

[which] I call out, and be gracious to
me and answer me.
8 On Your behalf, my heart says,
“Seek My presence.” Your presence,
O Lord, I will seek.
9 Do not hide Your presence from me;
do not turn Your servant away with
anger. You were my help; do not forsake me and do not abandon me, O
G-d of my salvation.
10 For my father and my mother have
forsaken me, but the Lord gathers me
in.
11 Instruct me, O Lord, in Your way,
and lead me in the straight path because of those who lie in wait for me.
12 Do not deliver me to the desires of
my adversaries, for false witnesses
and speakers of evil have risen against
me.
13 Had I not believed in seeing the
good of the Lord in the land of the
living!
14 Hope for the Lord, be strong and
He will give your heart courage, and
hope for the Lord.

Some commentators believe that David wrote this Psalm during a time when he was in trouble and when everything seemed dark. This Psalm has an important role in the Jewish liturgy and is customarily recited twice a day, starting a month before the Jewish New Year holiday, Rosh Hashanah. According to *The New Psalm: The Psalms as Literature* by Benjamin J. Segal, this Psalm appears to be written in two independent units. The first portion shows self-assurance. In the second portion, an enemy approaches. David asks G-d to have pity on him and not abandon him.

He also speaks about courage in this Psalm. In Verse 14, he urges us to "Hope for the Lord, be strong and he will give your heart courage..."

In my painting, the two candles symbolize the first Verse that states: "The Lord is my light." The light of the two candles shows the way forward against a dark and foreboding background.

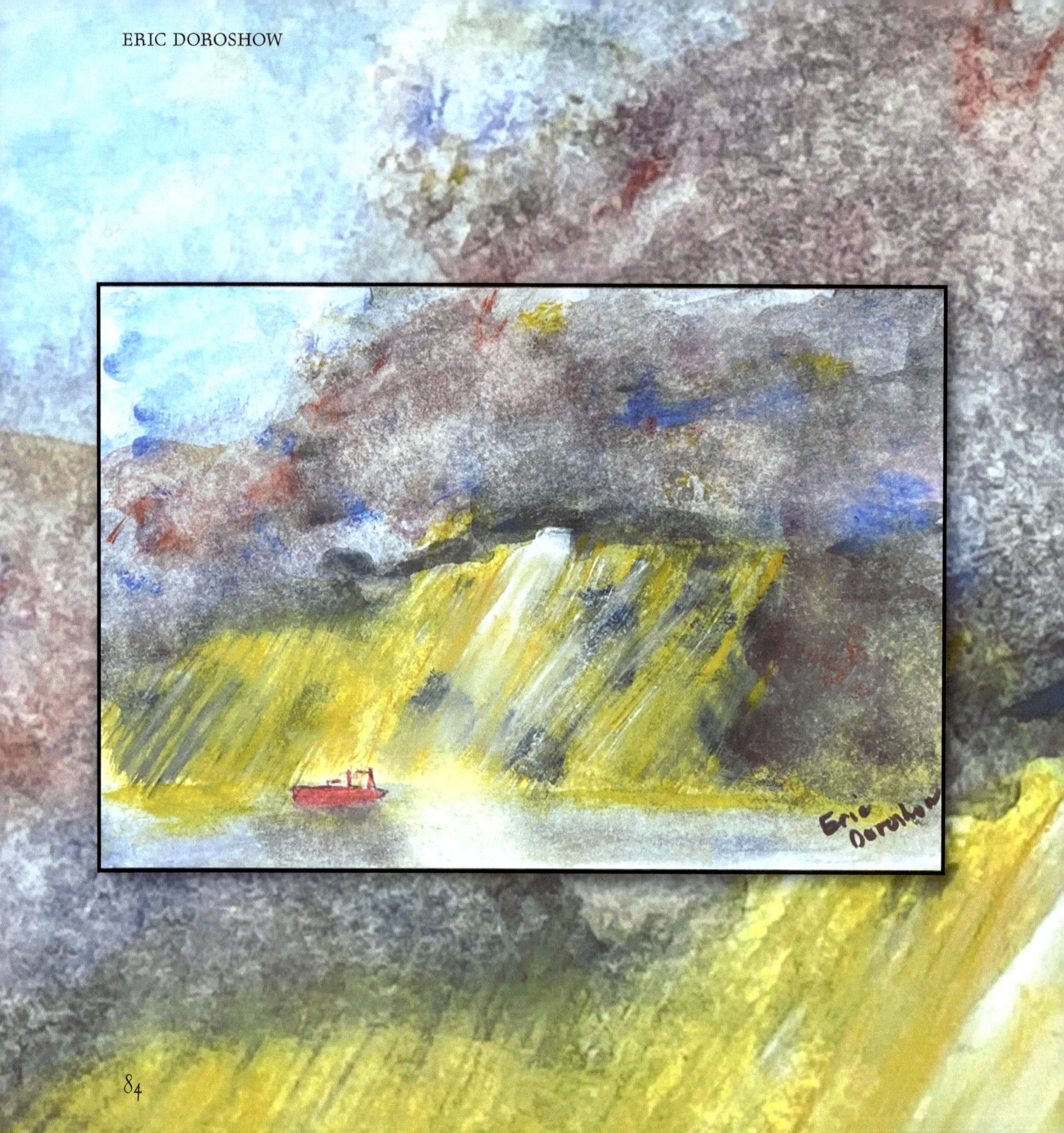
Eric
Doroshow

Psalm 29

1 A song of David. Prepare for the
Lord, [you] sons of the mighty; prepare for the Lord glory and might.
2 Prepare for the Lord the glory due
His name; prostrate yourselves to
the Lord in the place beautified with
sanctity.
3 The voice of the Lord is upon the
waters; the G-d of glory thunders; the
Lord is over the vast waters.
4 The voice of the Lord is in strength;
the voice of the Lord is in beauty.
5 The voice of the Lord breaks the cedars, yea, the Lord breaks the cedars
of Lebanon.
6 He causes them to dance like a calf,
Lebanon and Sirion like a young wild
ox.
7 The voice of the Lord cleaves with
flames of fire.
8 The voice of the Lord causes the
desert to quake; the Lord causes the
desert of Kadesh to quake.
9 The voice of the Lord will frighten the
hinds and strip the forests, and in His
Temple everyone speaks of His glory.

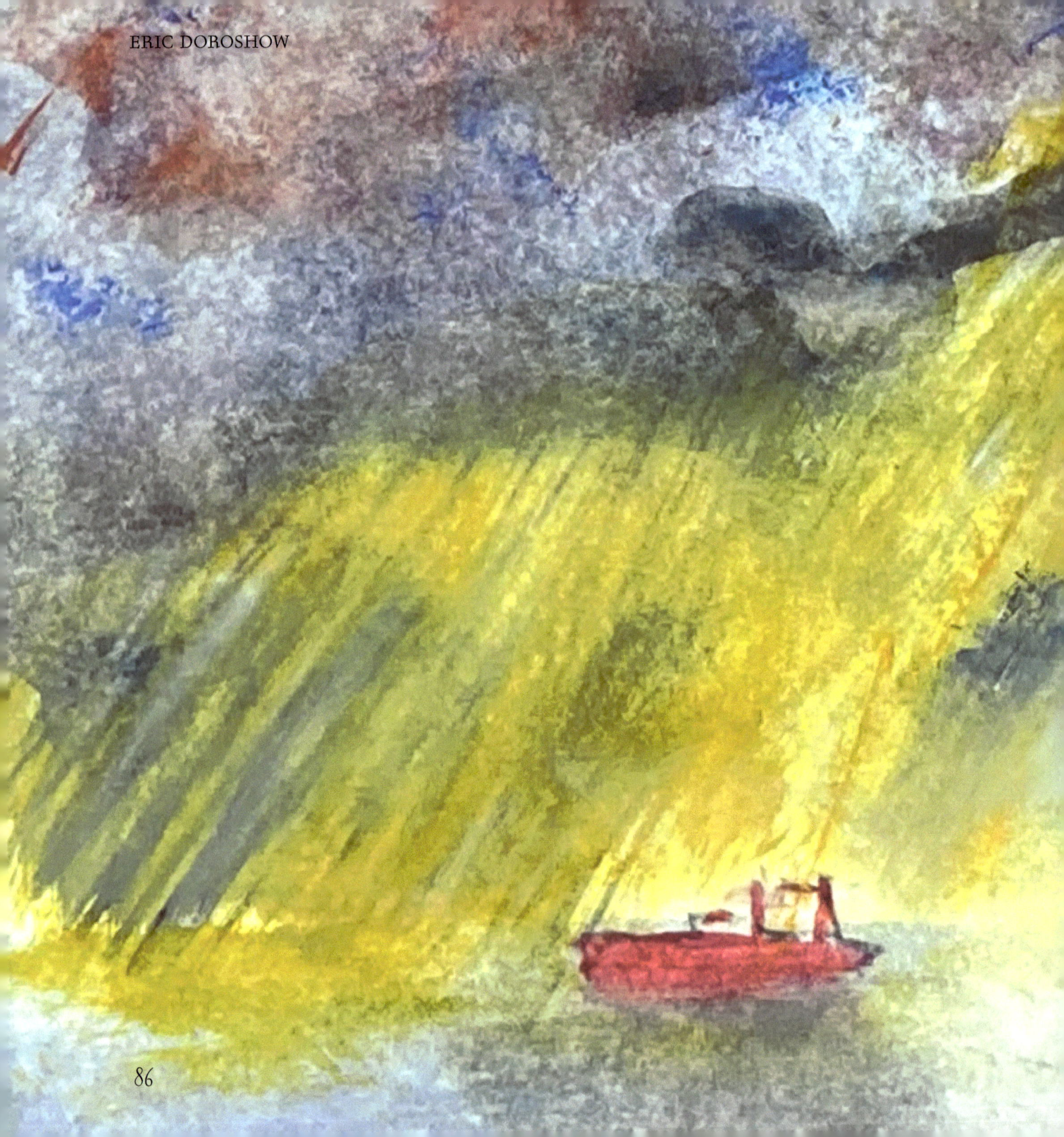

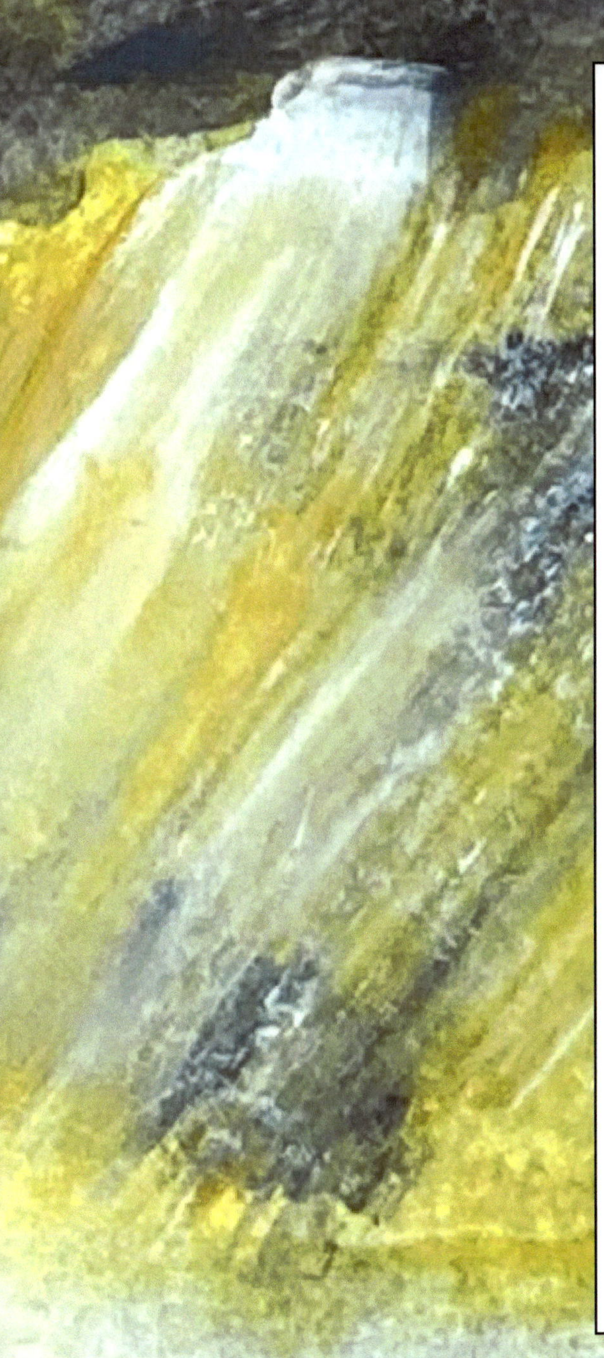

10 The Lord sat [enthroned] at the
flood; the Lord sat as King forever.
11 The Lord shall grant strength to
His people; the Lord shall bless His
people with peace.

Psalm 29 focuses almost exclusively on G-d and is filled with sharp visual images. It is a hymn describing the advent of G-d in a storm. It is recited during the Jewish Sabbath service when ceremonially returning the congregation's Torah to the Ark.

In my painting, Verse 3 is referenced. A small boat is shown navigating tumultuous waters during a storm. A shaft of light on the water symbolizes G-d.

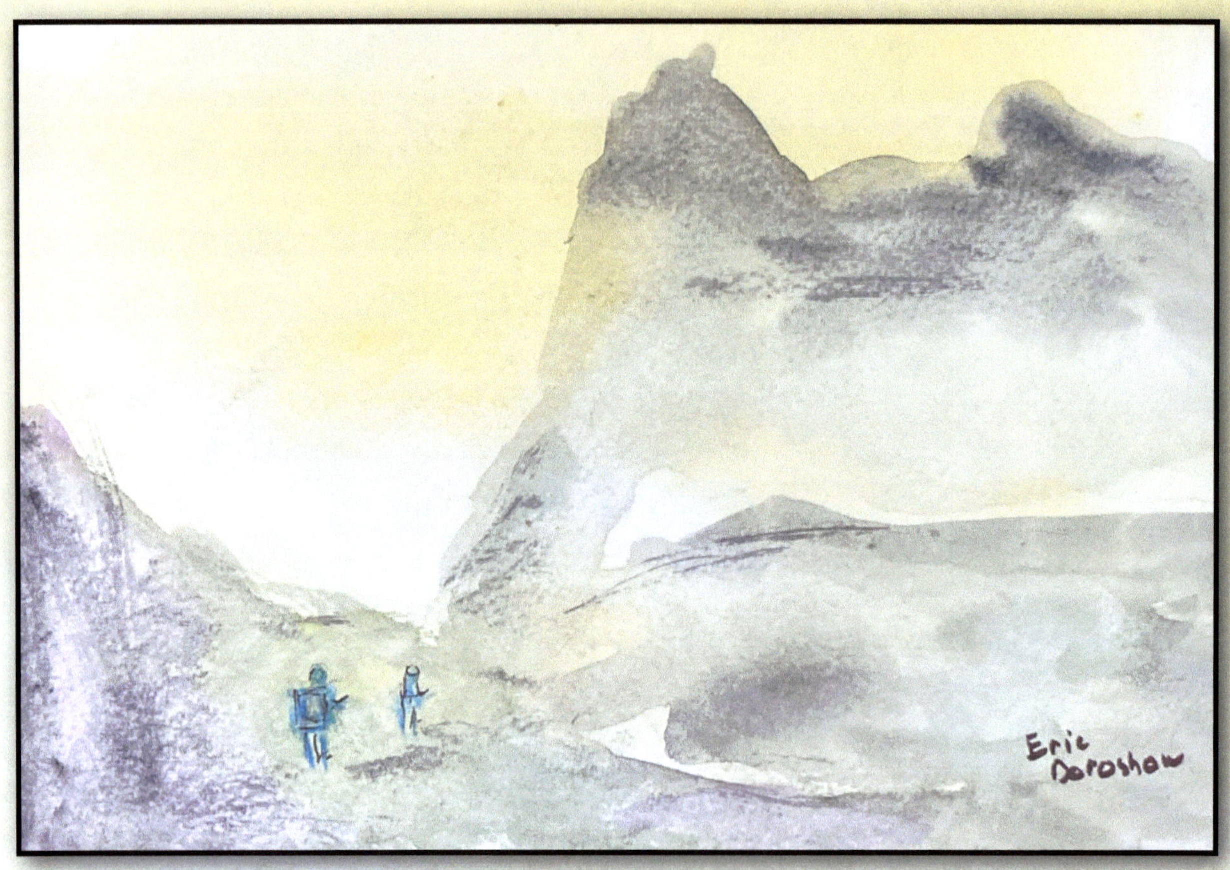
Eric
Doroshow

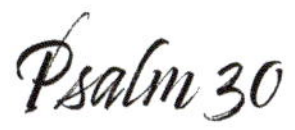

Psalm 30

1 A psalm; a song of dedication of the
House, of David.
2 I will exalt You, O Lord, for You
have raised me up, and You have not
allowed my enemies to rejoice over
me.
3 O Lord, I have cried out to You, and
You have healed me.
4 O Lord, You have brought my soul
from the grave; You have revived me
from my descent into the Pit.
5 Sing to the Lord, His pious ones,
and give thanks to His holy name.
6 For His wrath lasts but a moment;
life results from His favor; in the evening, weeping may tarry, but in the
morning there is joyful singing.
7 And I said in my tranquility, "I will
never falter."
8 O Lord, with Your will, You set
up my mountain to be might, You
hid Your countenance and I became
frightened.
9 To You, O Lord, I would call, and
to the Lord I would supplicate.
10 "What gain is there in my blood,

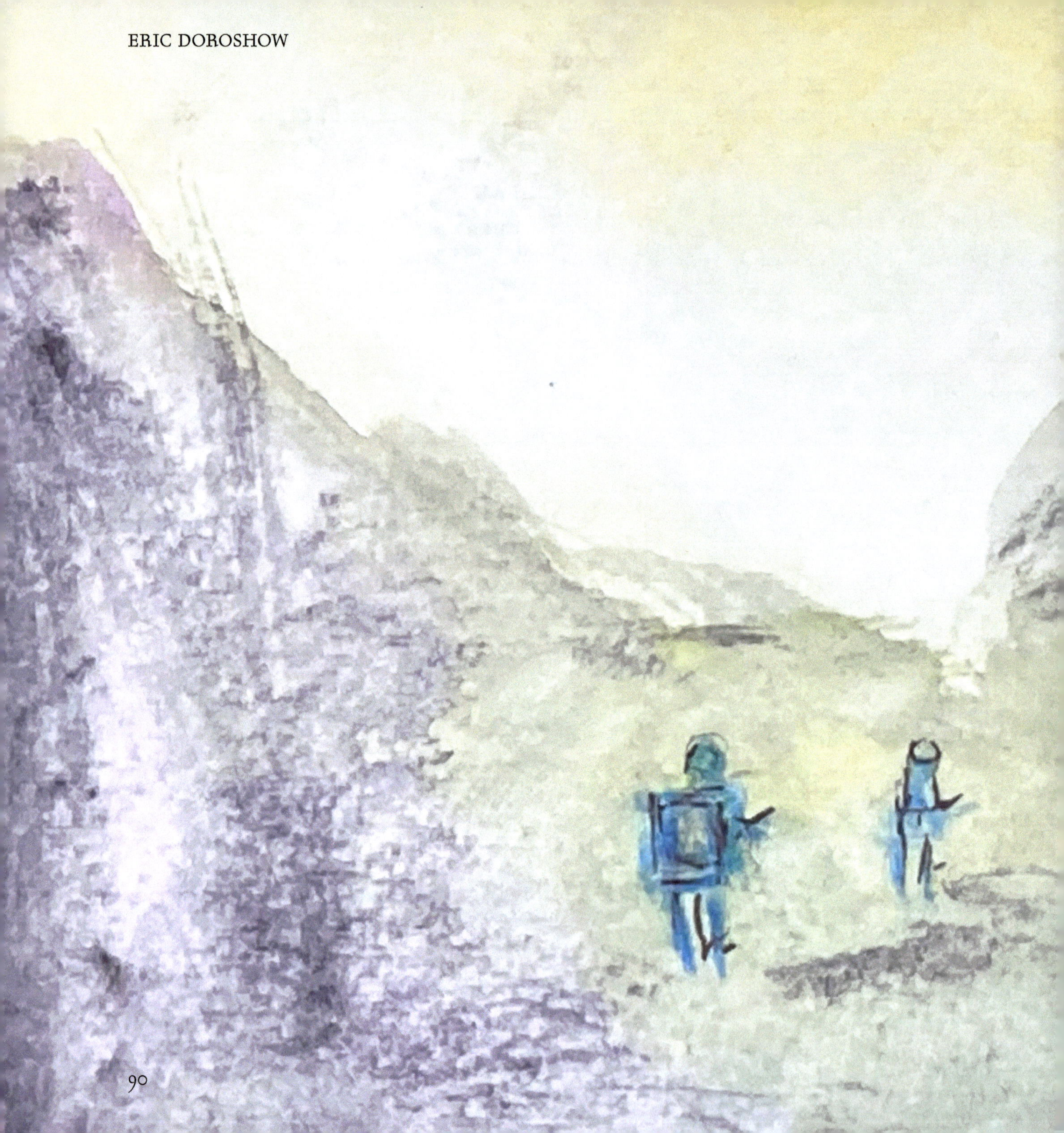

in my descent to the grave? Will dust
thank You; will it recite Your truth?
11 Hear, O Lord, and be gracious to
me; O Lord, be my helper."
12 You have turned my lament into
dancing for me; You loosened my
sackcloth and girded me with joy.
13 So that my soul will sing praises to
You and not be silent. O Lord, my
G-d, I will thank You forever.

Psalm 30 talks about a journey of someone who passes through a very frightening experience. At the end of the Psalm, the person emerges to thank G-d. This is a Psalm of thanksgiving, traditionally ascribed to David upon the building of his own royal palace. It is also customarily recited daily during the Jewish holiday of Hannukah.

In my painting, Verse 8 is referenced: "You set up my mountain to be might." Two figures are seen hiking in a mountain region during sunrise, surrounded by a yellow, spiritual light.

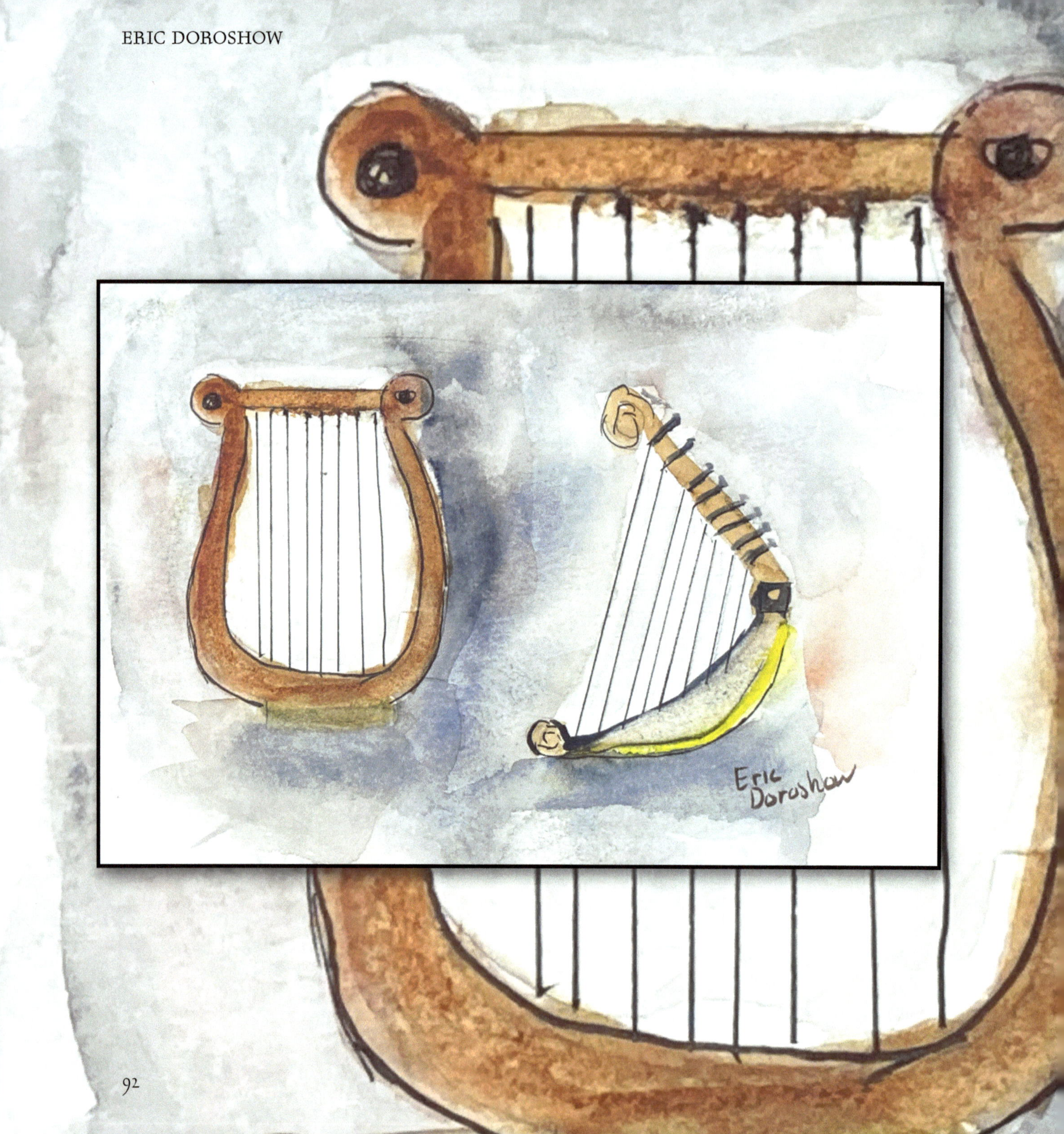
Eric
Doroshow

Psalm 108

1 A song, a psalm of David.
2 My heart is steadfast, O G-d; I shall
sing and play music, even my glory.
3 Awaken, you psaltery and harp; I
shall awaken the dawn.
4 I shall thank You among the peoples, O Lord, and I shall play music
to You among the kingdoms.
5 For Your kindness is great above the
heavens, and Your truth is until the
skies.
6 Lift Yourself above the heavens, O
Lord, and over all the earth is Your
glory.
7 In order that Your beloved ones be
released, save with Your right hand
and answer me.
8 G-d spoke in His holiness, that I
would rejoice, that I would allot a
portion, and that I would measure
the valley of Succoth.
9 Gilead is mine, Manasseh is mine,
and Ephraim is the strength of my
head; Judah is my prince.
10 Moab is my wash basin, on Edom I

shall cast my shoe; on Philistia I shall
shout.
11 Who will bring me to the fortified
city? He Who led me up to Edom?
12 Is it not You, O G-d, Who has forsaken us, and does not go, O Lord,
in our hosts?
13 Give us help against the adversary,
for man's salvation is futile.
14 With G-d we shall gather strength,
and He will trample our adversaries.

This Psalm contains references to the use of music as a method to give praise to G-d. In Verse 3, two musical instruments were mentioned: the psaltery (which is a stringed instrument similar to a lyre) and the harp. These ancient musical instruments used by David and are the subject of my watercolor.

In Chapter 6, I discussed David's musical talent. David had a reputation as a skillful player on the lyre in his youth. In I Samuel 16:16-23, it is written that the spirit of the Lord had departed from Saul and an evil spirit began to terrify him. He asked his attendants to find someone

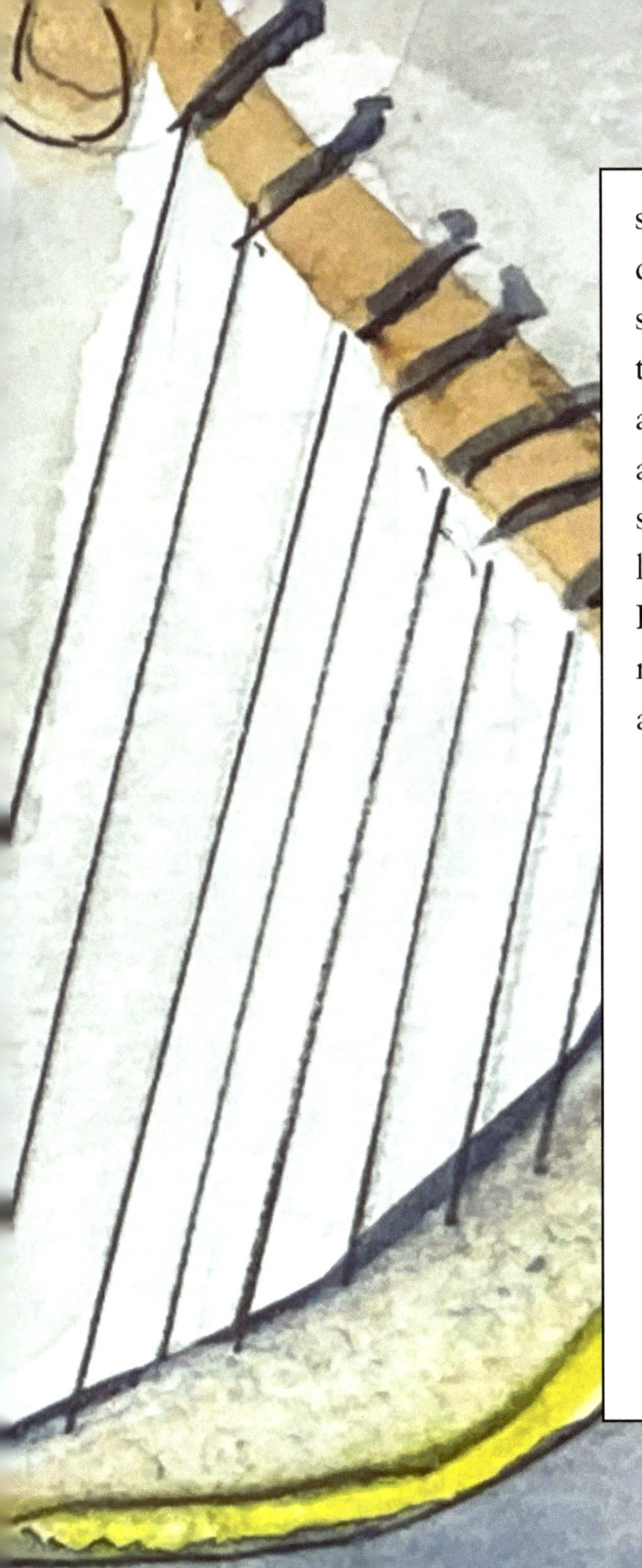

skilled in playing the lyre. One of Saul's attendants heard of David. He said, "Behold, I saw a son of Jesse the Bethlehemite, who knows how to play, a mighty man of valor, and a warrior, and prudent in affairs, and a handsome man, and the Lord is with him." Whenever the evil spirit came upon Saul, David would take to the lyre and play it, and Saul would find relief. When David brought the Ark of the Covenant into Jerusalem, he danced to the sounds of lyres, harps and other musical instruments II Samuel 6:30.

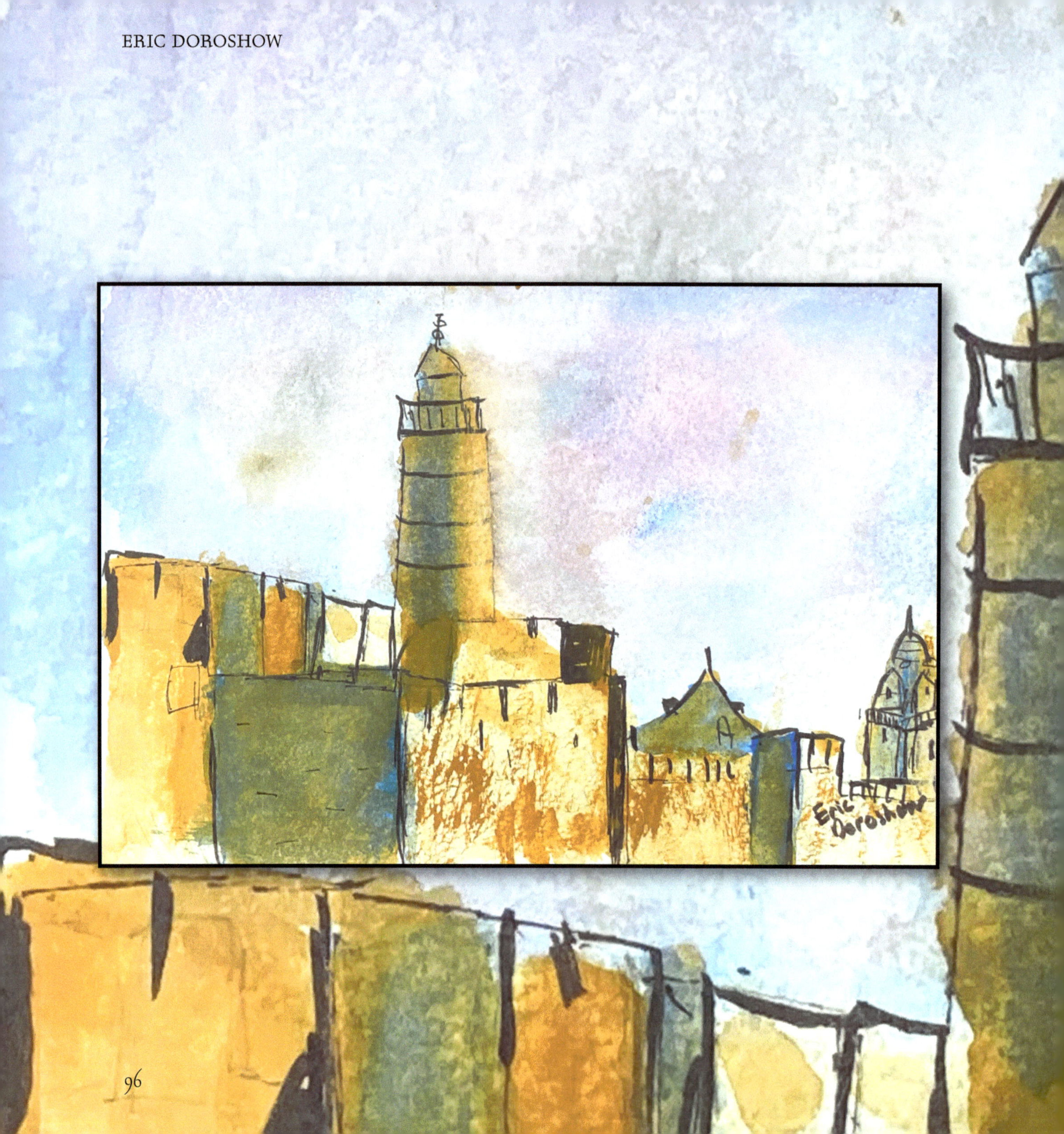
Eric Doroshow

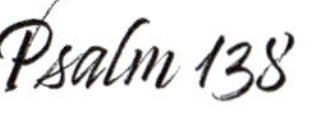

1 Of David. I shall thank You with all
my heart; before the princes I shall
you're your praises.
2 I shall prostrate myself toward Your
holy Temple, and I shall give thanks
to Your name for Your kindness and
for Your truth, for You magnified
Your word over all Your names.
3 On the day that I called and You
answered me; You made me great,
[putting] strength into my soul.
4 Lord, all the kings of the earth will
acknowledge You, for they heard the
words of Your mouth.
5 And they will sing of the ways of
the Lord for great is the glory of the
Lord.
6 For the Lord is high but He sees the
lowly, and He chastises the haughty
from afar.
7 If I walk in the midst of distress,You
revive me; against the wrath of my
enemies, You stretch forth Your hand
and Your right hand saves me.
8 May the Lord agree with me; O
Lord, may Your kindness be eternal.

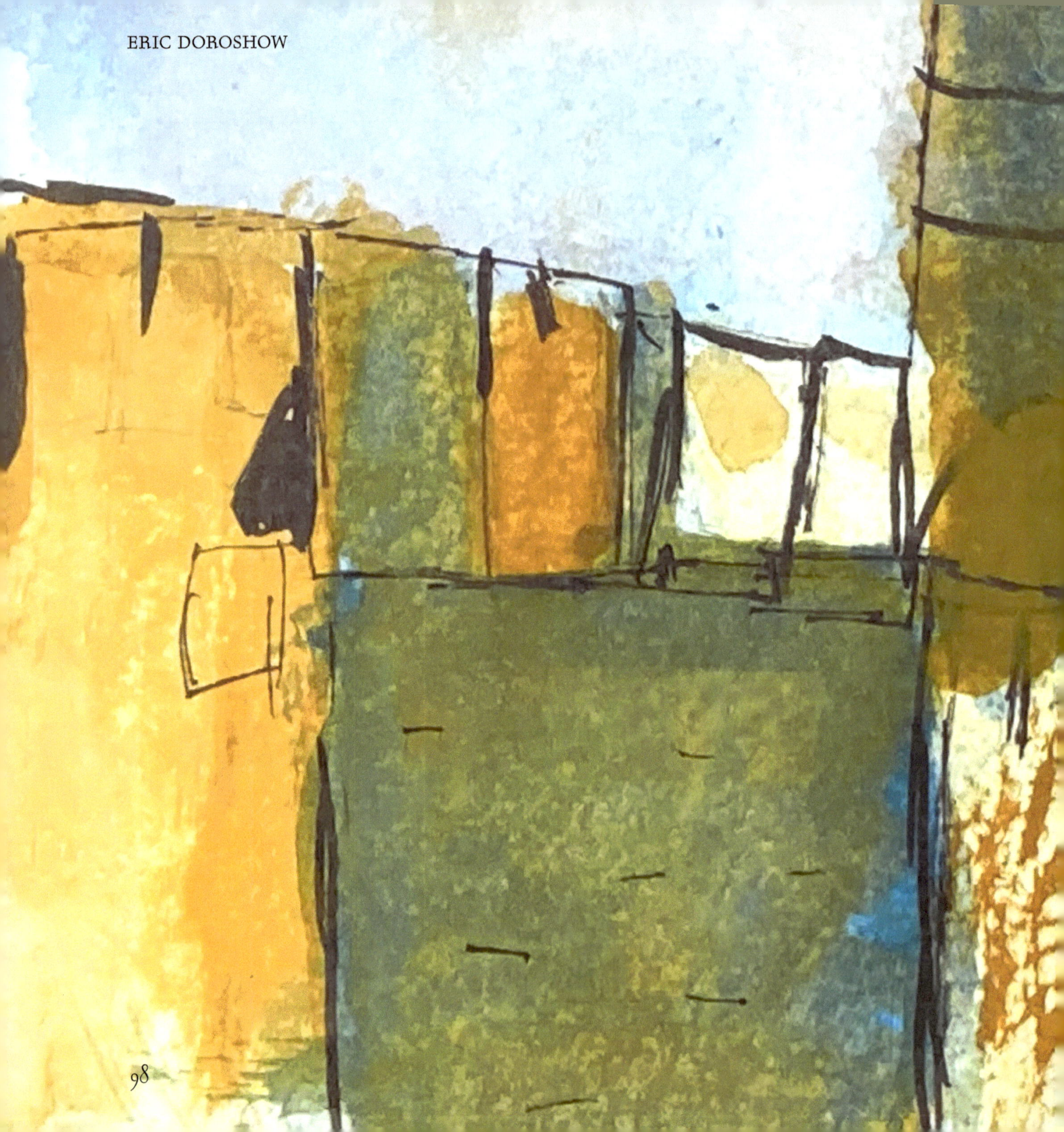

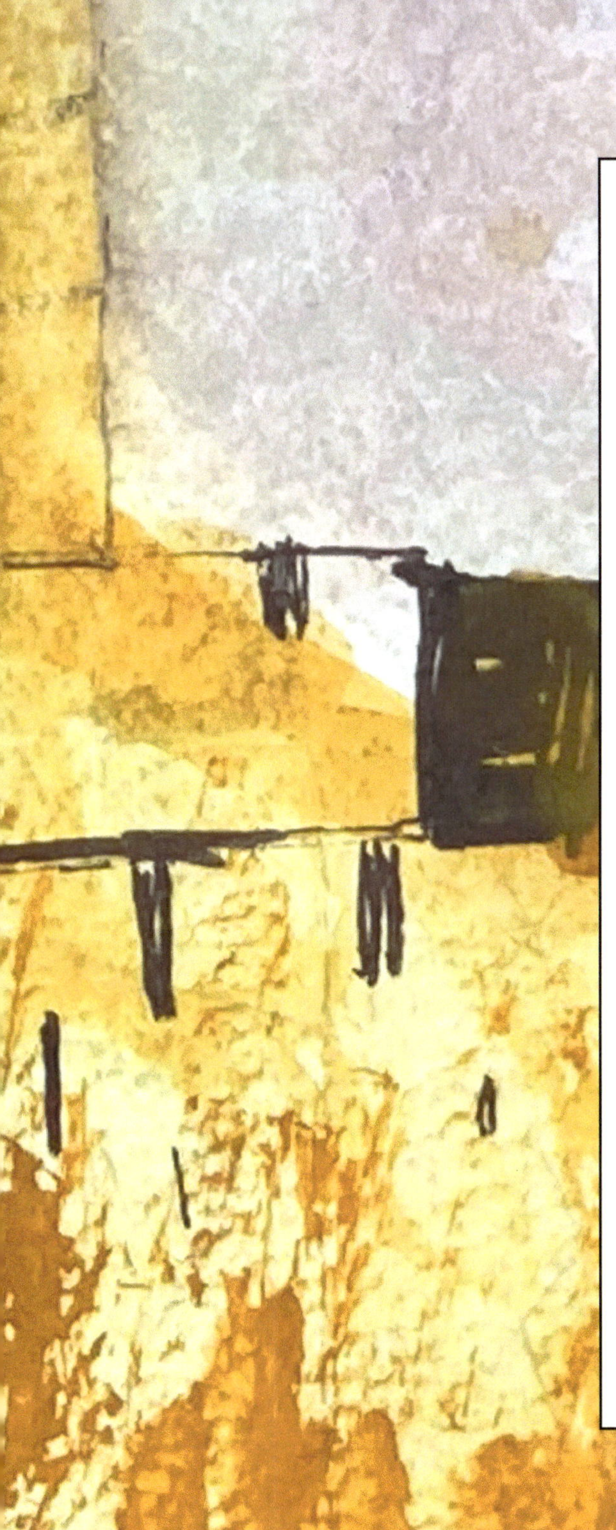

Do not let go of the works of Your hands.

Psalm 138 is traditionally recited as a Psalm of thanks and gratitude to G-d.

In Verse 2, the Psalm talks about bowing toward "your holy Temple." Many commentators believe that this was a reference to Jerusalem. As we have seen in earlier chapters, David had an important role in the establishment of Jerusalem as the religious and administrative center of ancient Israel.

In my painting, the towers around Jerusalem are depicted.

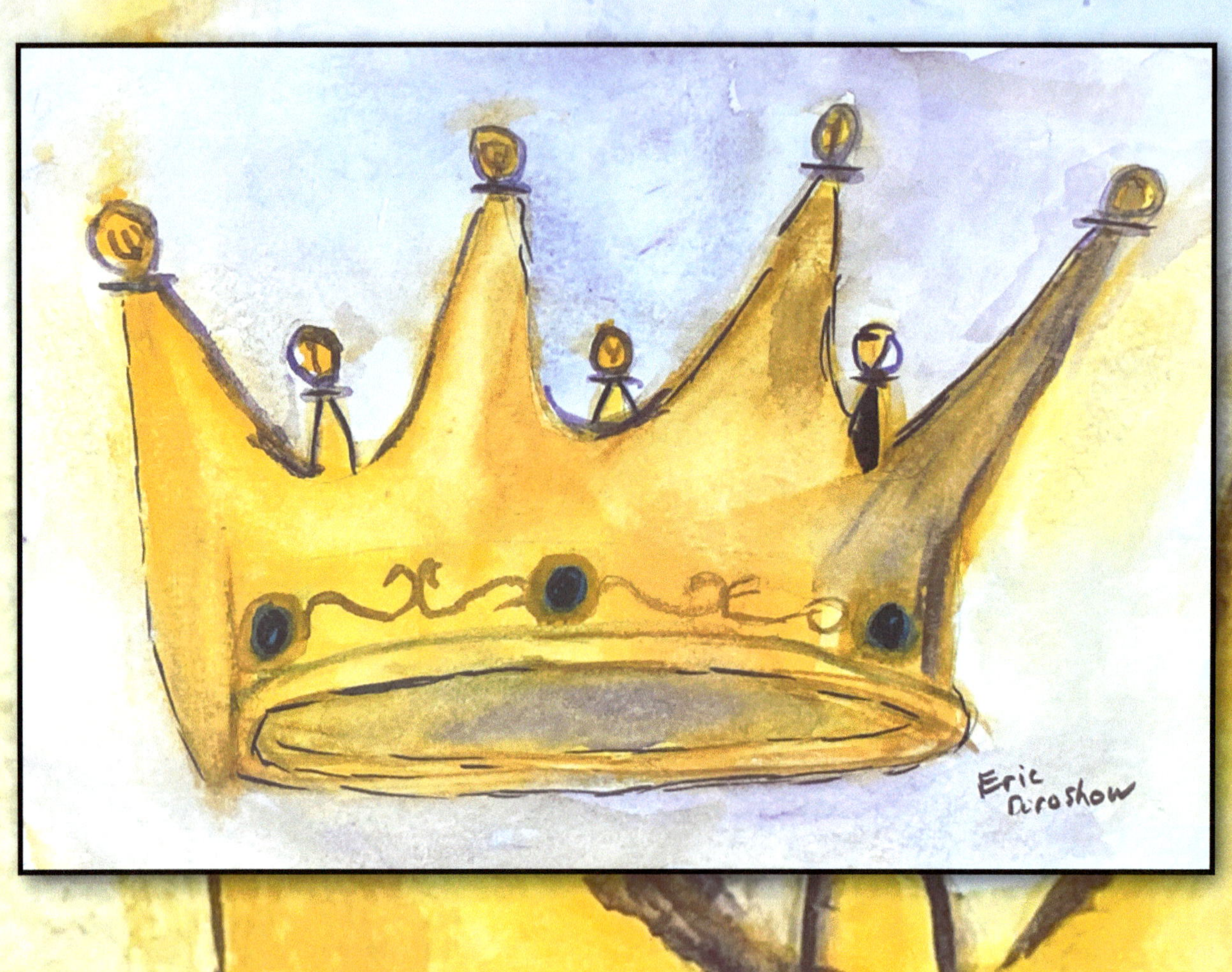
Eric
Doroshow

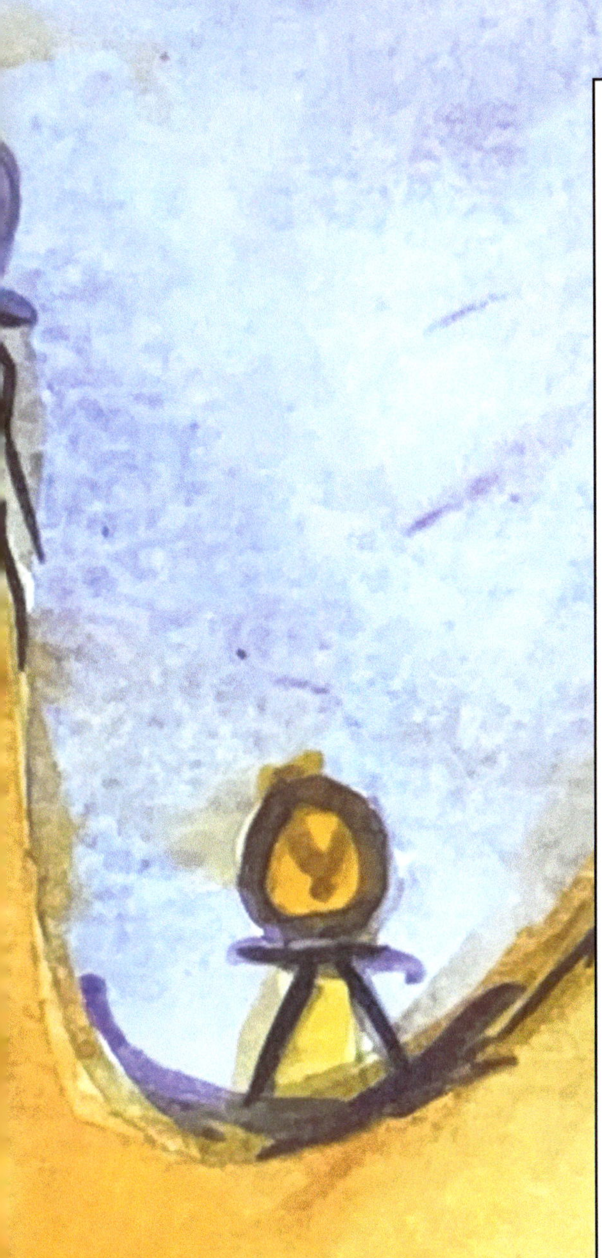

Psalm 145

1 A praise of David. I shall exalt You,
my G-d the King, and I shall bless
Your name forever and ever.
2 Every day I shall bless You, and I
shall praise Your name forever and
ever.
3 The Lord is great and very much
praised; and His greatness cannot be
searched.
4 Generation to generation will praise
Your works, and they will recite Your
mighty deeds.
5 Of the majesty of the glory of Your
splendor and the words of Your won-
ders I shall speak.
6 And the strength of Your awesome
deeds they will tell, and Your greatness I shall sing.
7 Of the remembrance of Your abun-
dant goodness they will speak, and
of Your righteousness they will sing.
8 The Lord is gracious and compassionate, slow to anger and of great
kindness.
9 The Lord is good to all, and His
mercies are on all His works.

[10] All Your works will thank You, O
Lord, and Your pious ones will bless
You.
[11] They will tell the glory of Your
kingdom, and they will speak of Your
might.
[12] To make known to the children of
men His mighty deeds and the glory
of the majesty of His kingdom.
[13] Your kingdom is a kingdom of all
times, and Your ruling is in every
generation.
[14] The Lord supports all those who
fall and straightens all who are bent
down.
[15] Everyone's eyes look to You with
hope, and You give them their food
in its time.
[16] You open Your hand and satisfy every living thing [with] its desire.
[17] The Lord is righteous in all His
ways, and kind in all His deeds.
[18] The Lord is near to all who call
Him, to all who call Him with
sincerity.
[19] He does the will of those who fear
Him, and He hears their cry and
saves them.

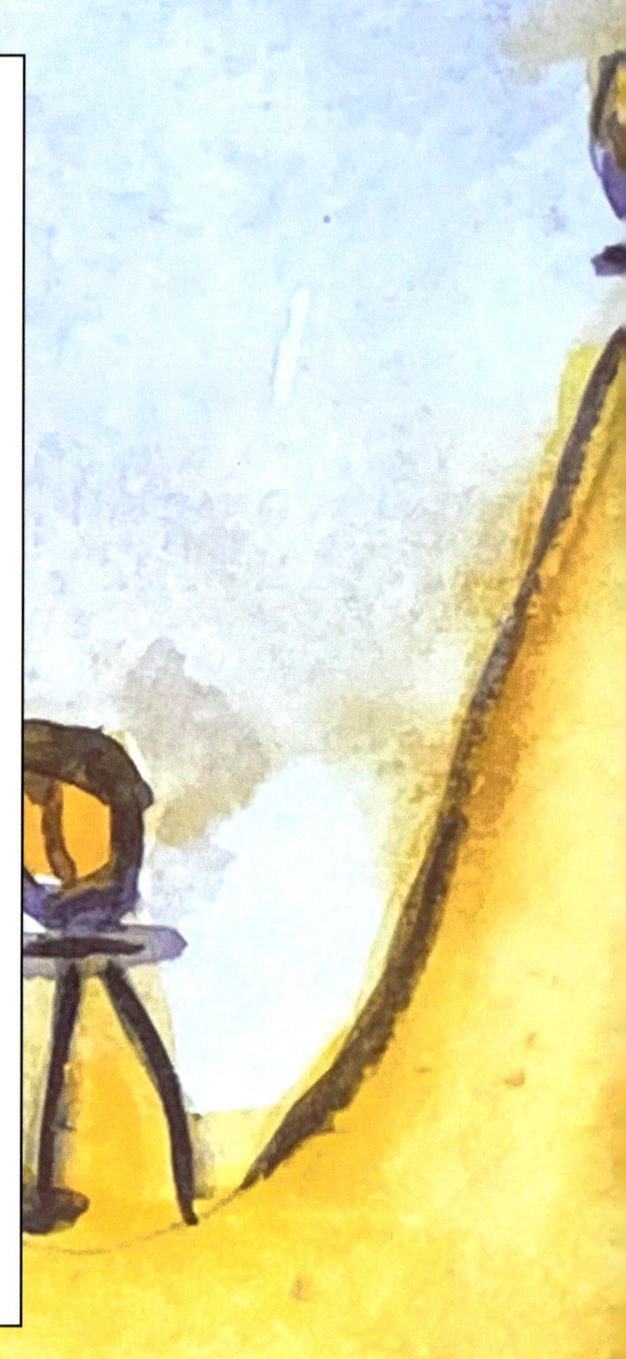

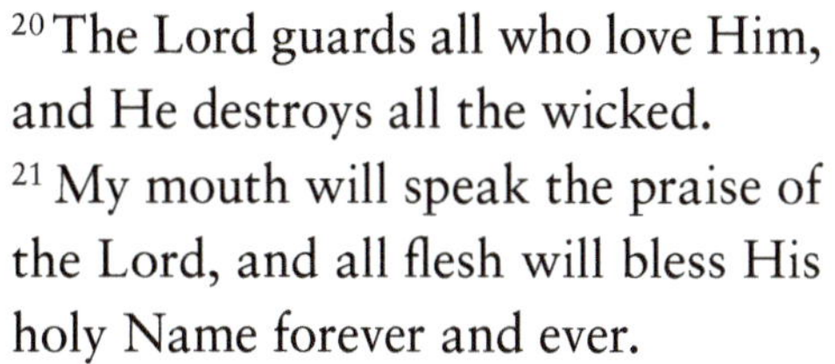

20 The Lord guards all who love Him,
and He destroys all the wicked.
21 My mouth will speak the praise of
the Lord, and all flesh will bless His
holy Name forever and ever.

This Psalm is the only Psalm labeled as a song of praise. It is the last Psalm attributed to David. According to *The New Psalm: The Psalms as Literature* by Benjamin J. Segal, this was the first Psalm incorporated in the post-Temple liturgy. It was a very important Psalm. According to the Talmud (which is a body of Jewish law and legend) if it was recited every day, it guaranteed eternal life.

In my watercolor, I refer to Verse 1 where G-d is referenced as King.

NOTES:

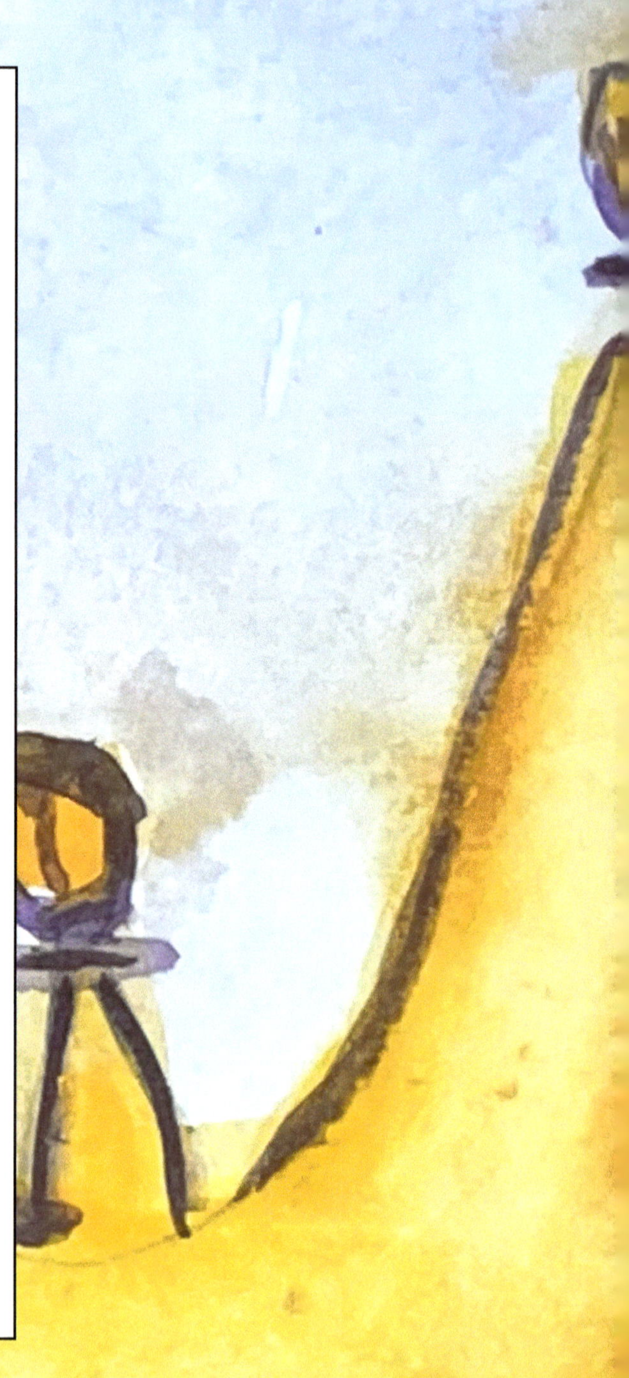

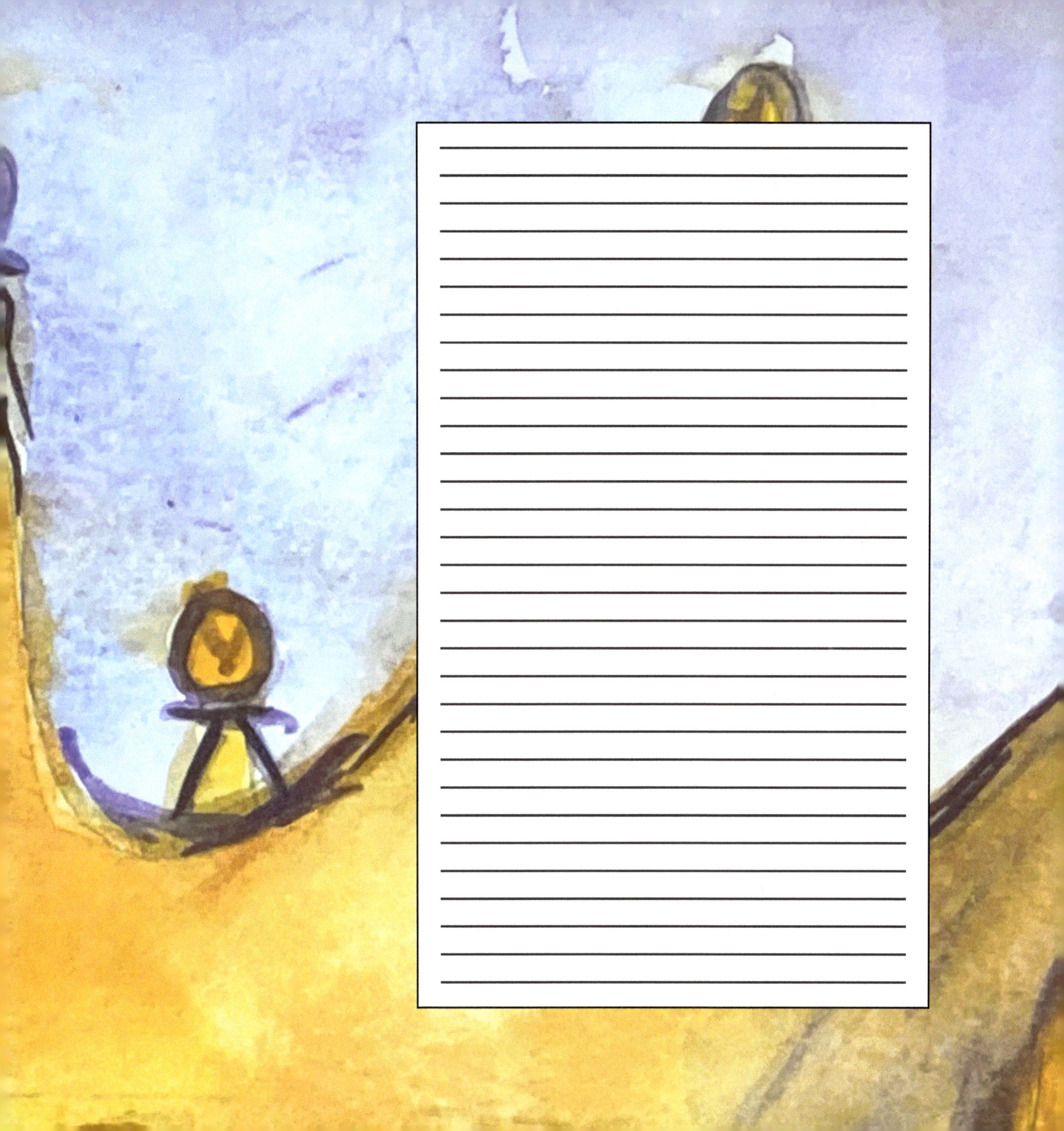

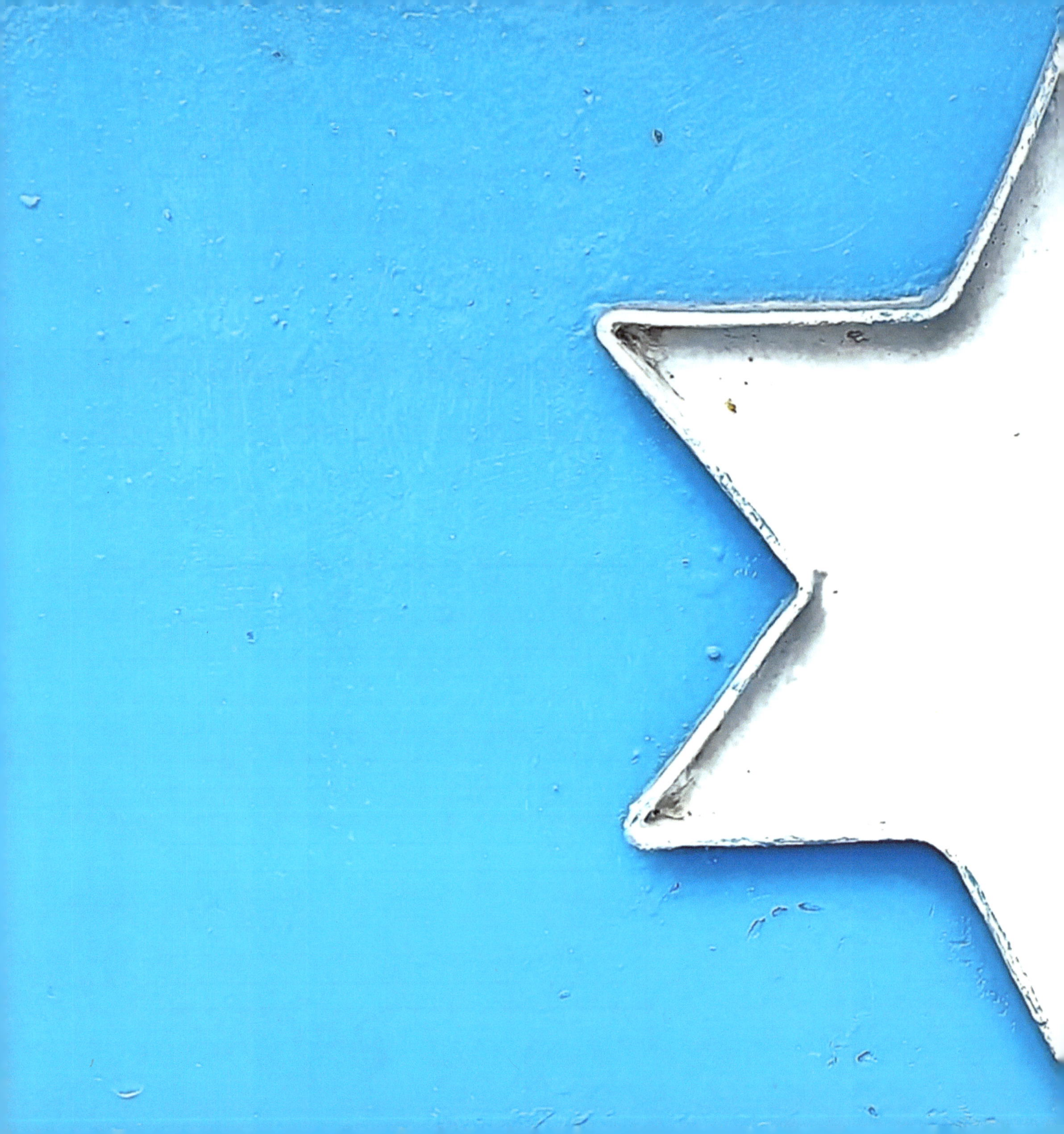

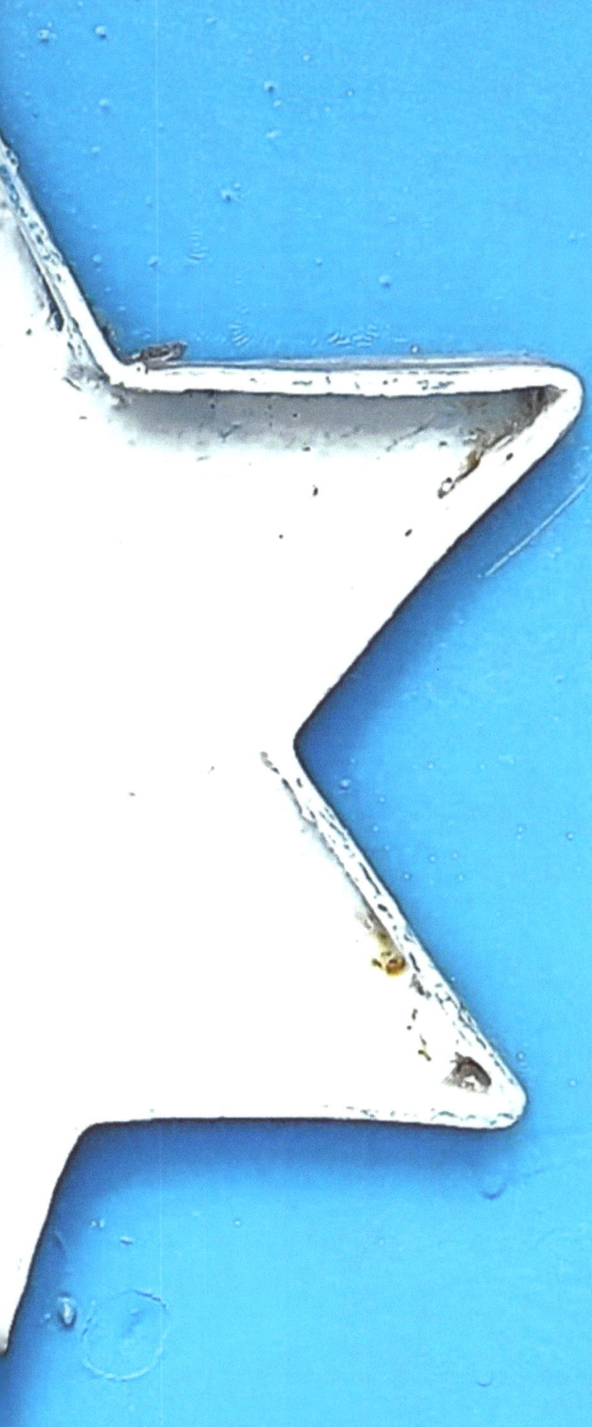

CHAPTER TEN

Why David's Story Is Relevant To Us Today

HOW CAN SOMEONE who lived over 3,000 years ago be relevant to our struggles today? If we distill the King David story down to the basics, we can benefit from learning about his personal qualities. These qualities have been applied to the stressful situations that people have dealt with throughout history.

As a Master Certified Life Coach and an Attorney, I work with people in all walks of life who are dealing with stressful situations. During my life coaching sessions, my clients and I discuss and apply the qualities that David exhibited to deal with life's most serious challenges. In this chapter, I'll discuss some of these qualities and show how you can apply them.

Perseverance

Perseverance means keeping our focus and effort on pursing a goal and sticking with it, even when we encounter obstacles and setbacks. We have been told many times that when we get knocked down, we need to get back up and try again. Various commentators have written that perseverance is an essential quality for success in life. In King David's story, we see examples of his perseverance again and again. David had to deal with challenges to his power from far stronger enemies, his own people, and even his own family. He did not give up when he was confronted with these challenges. He demonstrated perseverance when he killed Goliath, expanded a united Israel, and made Jerusalem the center of his kingdom. We can confront today's challenges by following his example.

Courage

Courage, in the purest sense, is an individual trait that must be summoned in times of extreme stress. When we show courage, it is often infectious and brings others who are less courageous across the line as well.

We spent all of Chapter 3 talking about the numerous ways David showed courage. We have seen how his courage was infectious to others. David's showed courage by battling his enemies, both internal and external. As a result, he helped the Kingdom of Israel to survive and thrive. We can take his lessons of courage and apply them today when we are confronted with tough times.

Humility

In the Jewish philosophical study called Mussar, humility plays an important part in living a good life. It unveils a self-awareness and an honest assessment of who you are. *Everyday Holiness, The Jewish Spiritual Path of Musar* by Alan Morinis (2011 Trumpeter Books). Humility requires you to make an honest assessment of your life. With this honest assessment, you can move forward to successfully confront life's challenges. Conversely, those persons who do not have humility are often puffed up with arrogance and self-importance, and may have trouble honestly

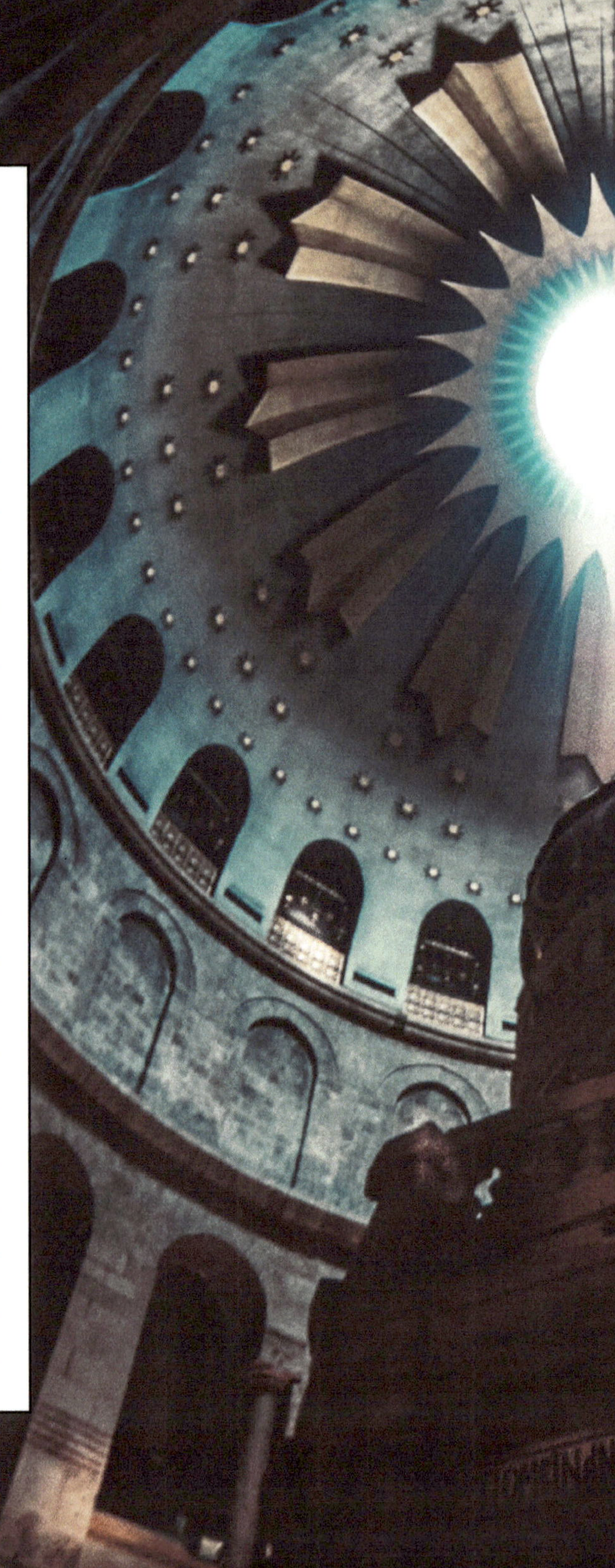

assessing their lives. In difficult times, humility serves us well. It keeps our egos balanced as we deal with stressful situations.

King David possessed humility. He started his life as a simple shepherd and rose to be King, yet he was always humble in his dealings. He made an accurate evaluation of himself, never making himself too grand. As we have seen in Chapter 9, his Psalms are often centered around his own inadequacies as a person. On numerous occasions, he humbly asked for G-d's forgiveness for his misdeeds.

Truthfulness

If we are going to successfully confront today's challenges, we must be truthful both to ourselves and those around us. We must use accurate speech in our dealings with others. There are many reasons why we might want to lie. Perhaps because we fear facing disappointment, fear, shame, or loss. We may wish to protect ourselves with a lie. The simple fact is that lying can damage us and those around us. Without truthfulness, we can't really confront our everyday challenges.

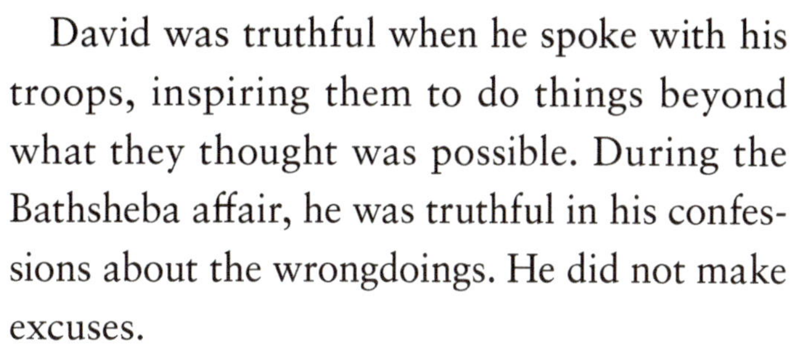

David was truthful when he spoke with his troops, inspiring them to do things beyond what they thought was possible. During the Bathsheba affair, he was truthful in his confessions about the wrongdoings. He did not make excuses.

Equanimity

Equanimity is a trait that demonstrates serenity and peacefulness. It is not tranquility which could be used to blot out the difficulties in life's challenges. It is keeping your cool when stressful things are happening all around you. The Mussar masters teach us that we must deal directly with life's challenges to thrive, but in doing so, we need to always keep an even keel. We must not get too high or too low.

As he had to confront many stressful situations, David demonstrated this trait many times during his life. These situations included battling Goliath, running from King Saul (who tried to kill him numerous times), and defending his kingship from usurpers in his family. He kept his wits about him and always seemed to find a way to deal with each challenge that was presented to him.

What is a good visual of equanimity? Think of a surfer calmly navigating waves that are crashing around him. The surfer is certainly aware of the dangers of the crashing waves, but he keeps his balance and focus in spite of those dangers. Without question, this is a very important trait that we can use to confront today's challenges.

Gratitude

Practicing gratitude means being fully aware of the good that already surrounds you. Despite all hardships that you can face in life, there is always something for which to be grateful. Gratitude helps you to discover how much good is in your life and changes your perspective on life's obstacles.

In *The Book of Joy: Lasting Happiness in a Changing World* (Random House, 2016), The Dalai Lama and Desmond Tutu wrote about the importance of recognizing joy and showing gratitude in everyday life. In the book, they show

how to transform gratitude, joy, and humor from fleeting emotions to a foundational way of life.

On numerous occasions, David expressed gratitude to G-d for his lot in life. His Psalms are full of gratitude for G-d and exemplify how we can apply these lessons of gratitude as we confront life's challenges.

Responsibility

Another way to confront life's challenges is to take responsibility for the errors we make. We must truthfully consider the consequences of our actions and take responsibility for the outcome. Shading the truth is counterproductive in our efforts to deal with these challenges. In other words: if you make a mess, clean it up.

David showed many instances of taking responsibility for his misdeeds. Unlike Saul, who blamed others for his misfortunes, David took responsibility for his mistakes. This made him a strong leader and helped him cope with the crises in his life.

By taking responsibility for our actions, we can go a long way toward correcting our mistakes. This, in turn, helps us to deal with life's challenges.

Order

Being organized in our lives is an important step in dealing with life's struggles. Sometimes we are overloaded with challenges from all sides. Whether it's family or work related, staying organized is an important skill we can use in dealing with these challenges in our lives. In fact, some commentators believe that disorder may be a reflection of internal disarray.

As we have seen in earlier chapters, David brought order to a disparate group of twelve tribes that did not have a cohesive leader. He made administrative districts out of each tribe to bring further order during his reign. This resulted in a cohesive nation that prospered.

We can take David's lessons to bring order into our own lives as we deal with life's challenges.

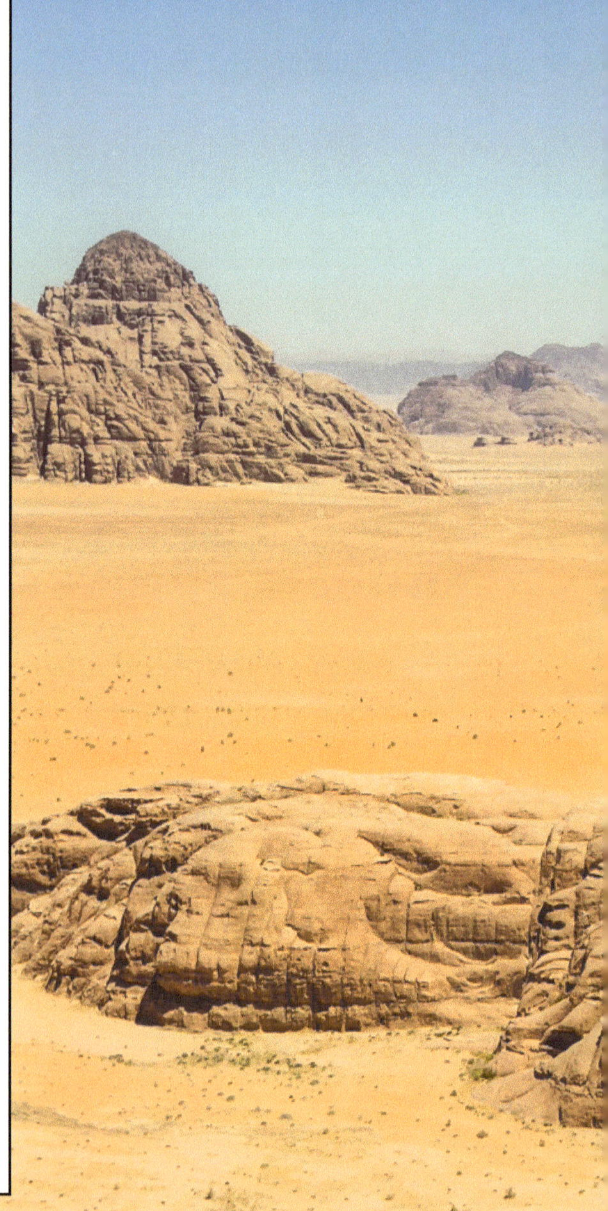

NOTES:

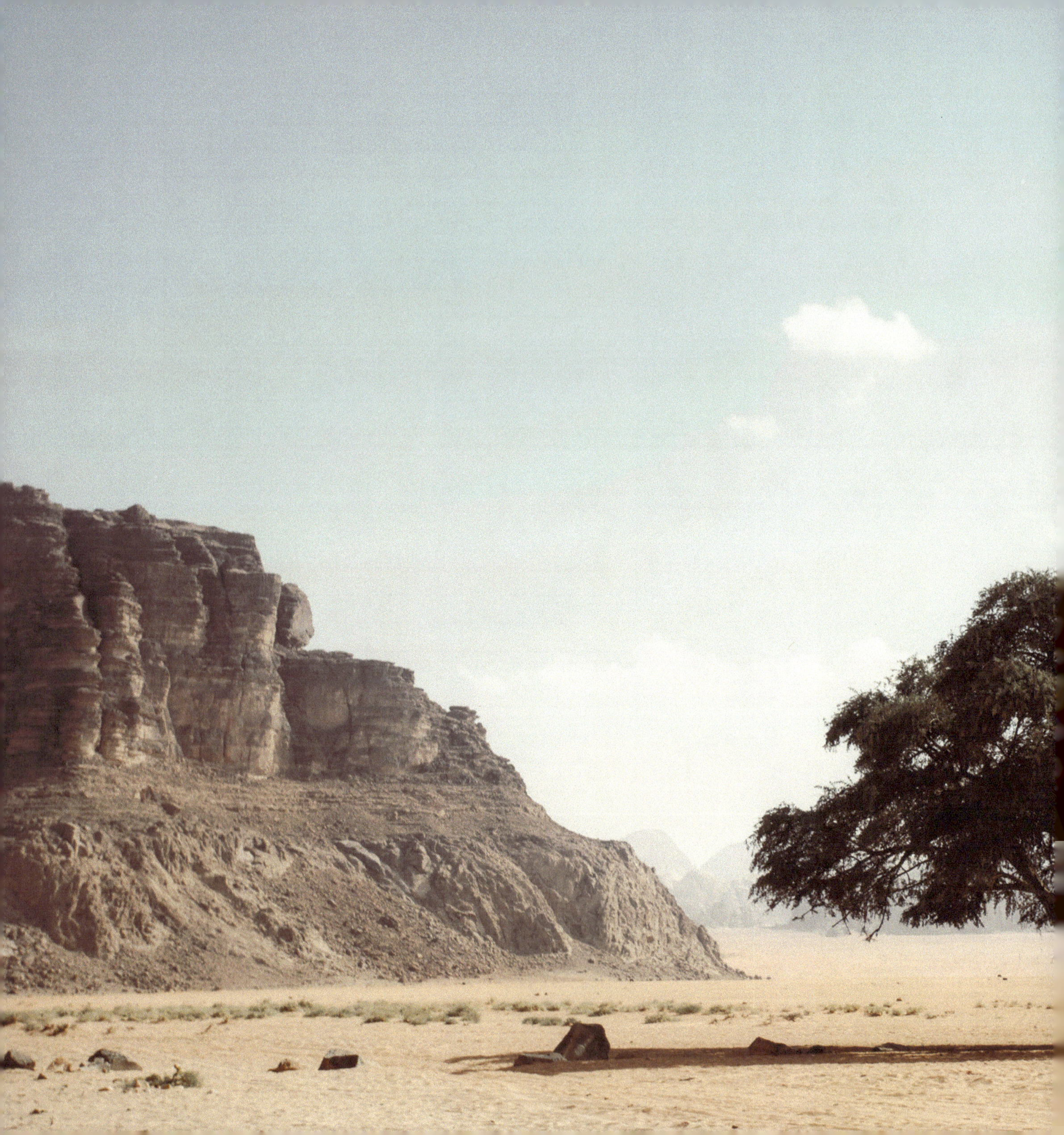

CONCLUSION

WE HAVE COME TO THE END of our discussion about David. As we have seen, the ancient story of David and his Psalms is relevant to us today in many ways. I hope that the paintings, along with the information in the book, gives you courage and inspiration to prosper in these troubled times.

ERIC M. DOROSHOW

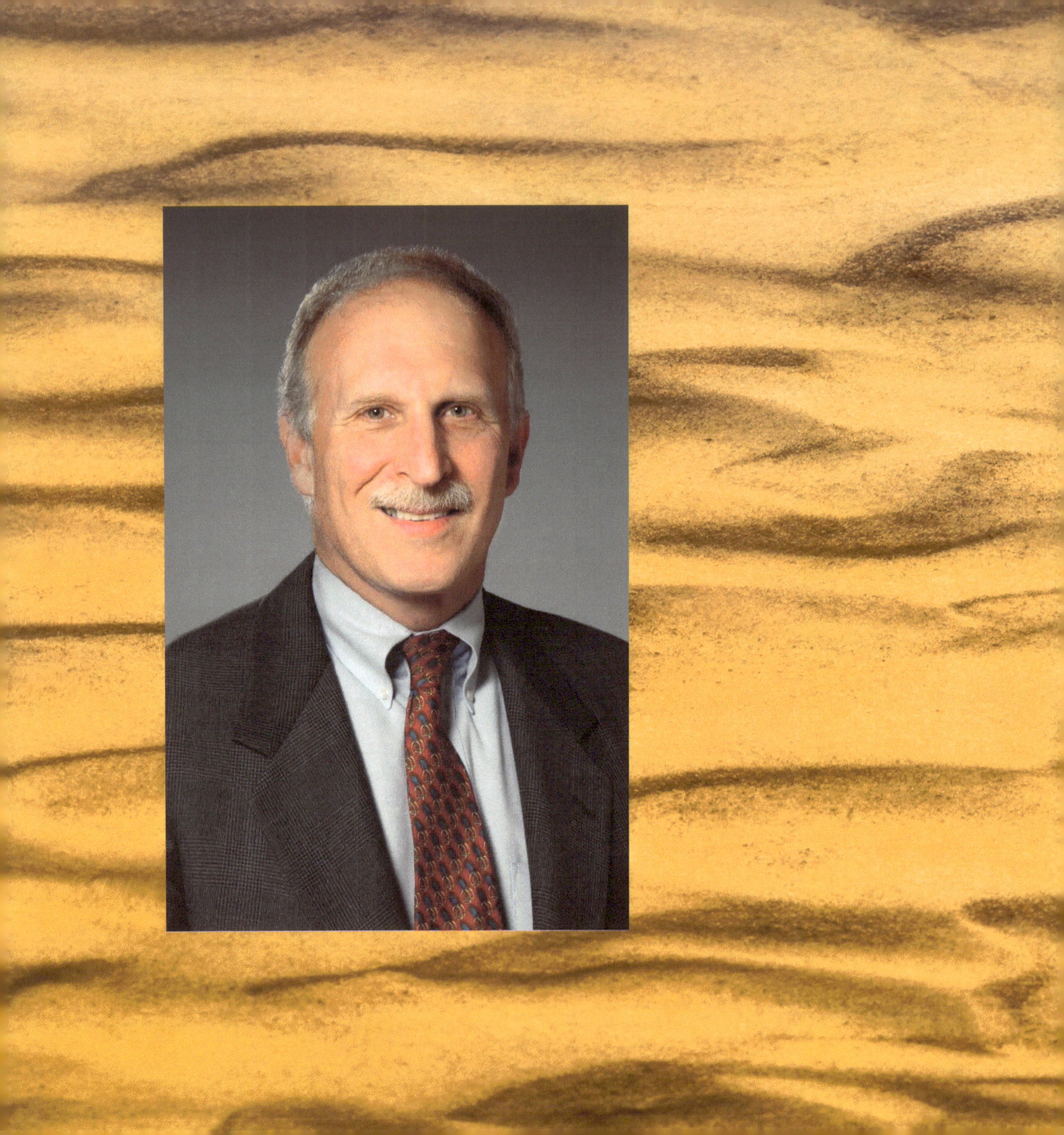

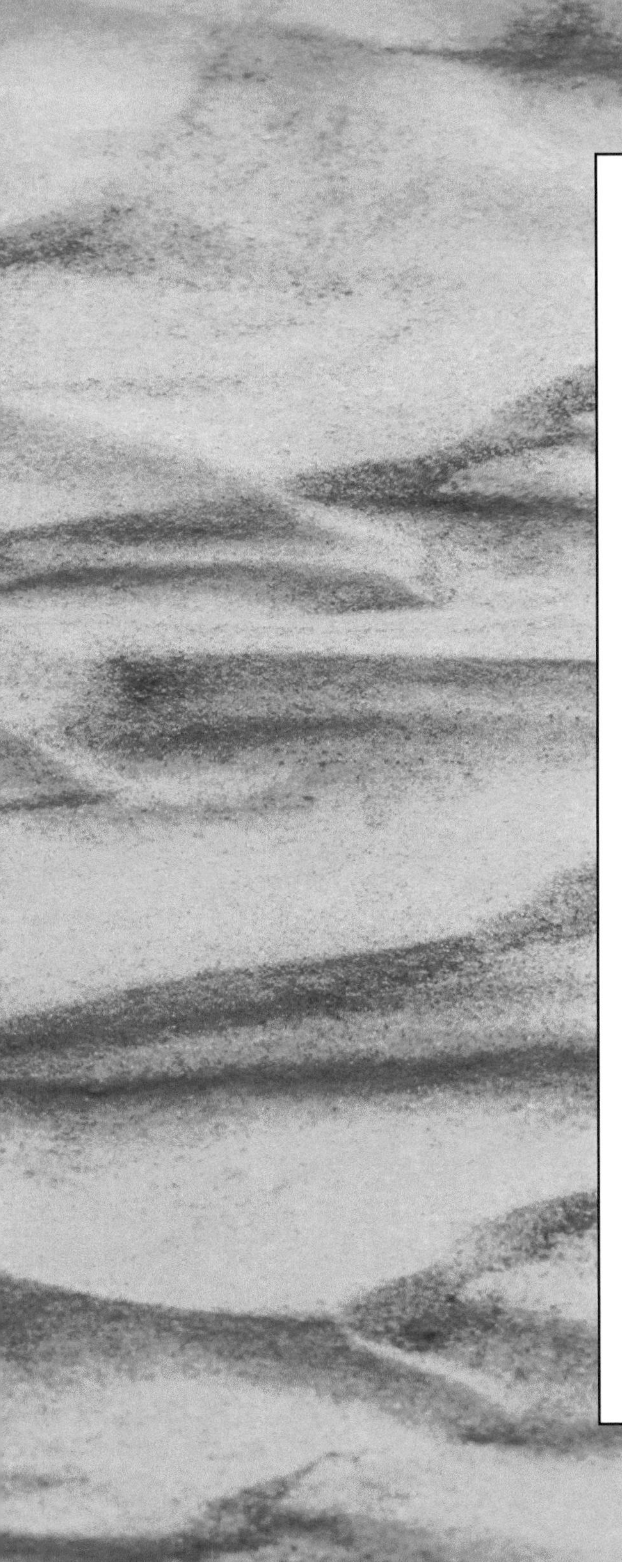

About the Author & Artist

Eric M. Doroshow is an attorney, artist, author, and life coach.

In his legal career, he is one of the founding partners of the Delaware law firm of Doroshow, Pasquale, Krawitz and Bhaya. He is a Past President of the Delaware Trial Lawyers Association. He is also a certified Arbitrator and Mediator in the Delaware Courts.

In his artistic career, he has been painting water-colors for several years. Although he has no formal artistic training, he has taken numerous classes and workshops with well-known Delaware artists.

In his career as an author, he has written and published two other books. His first book is entitled *The Twelve Tribes of Israel: An Artistic and Historical Journey.* That book is illustrated with 12 of his original watercolors, representing each one of the Twelve Tribes of Israel. His second book is entitled *The Delaware Auto Accident Book: Avoid the Mistakes That Can Wreck Your Injury Case.*

In his career as a life coach, he received a Master Certified Life Coach certification. He works with young professionals and entrepreneurs to help them achieve their personal and professional dreams and aspirations.

Eric can be reached at his office at 1202 Kirkwood Highway, Wilmington DE 19805. (302) 998-0100. His e-mail is: ericd@dplaw.com. Eric's website is: www.imagesinspired.net.

www.ingramcontent.com/pod-product-compliance
Lightning Source LLC
LaVergne TN
LVHW070213110826
845147LV00003B/569

* 9 7 9 8 2 1 8 0 9 8 6 7 4 *